T0328767

Cambridge Elements ≡

Elements in Music Since 1945
edited by
Mervyn Cooke
University of Nottingham

OLIVIER MESSIAEN'S
TURANGALÎLA-SYMPHONIE

Andrew Shenton
Boston University

CAMBRIDGE
UNIVERSITY PRESS

Shaftesbury Road, Cambridge CB2 8EA, United Kingdom

One Liberty Plaza, 20th Floor, New York, NY 10006, USA

477 Williamstown Road, Port Melbourne, VIC 3207, Australia

314–321, 3rd Floor, Plot 3, Splendor Forum, Jasola District Centre, New Delhi – 110025, India

103 Penang Road, #05–06/07, Visioncrest Commercial, Singapore 238467

Cambridge University Press is part of Cambridge University Press & Assessment, a department of the University of Cambridge.

We share the University's mission to contribute to society through the pursuit of education, learning and research at the highest international levels of excellence.

www.cambridge.org
Information on this title: www.cambridge.org/9781009165730

DOI: 10.1017/9781009165723

First published 2023

A catalogue record for this publication is available from the British Library.

ISBN 978-1-009-16573-0 Paperback
ISSN 2632-7791 (online)
ISSN 2632-7783 (print)

Additional resources for this publication at www.cambridge.org/Shenton

Olivier Messiaen's *Turangalîla-symphonie*

Elements in Music Since 1945

DOI: 10.1017/9781009165723
First published online: September 2023

Andrew Shenton
Boston University
Author for correspondence: Andrew Shenton, shenton@bu.edu

Abstract: As one of only a few pieces not primarily inspired by Messiaen's Catholic faith, but by human love as described in the romance of Tristan and Isolde and elsewhere, the *Turangalîla-symphonie* is contextualized in Messiaen's oeuvre and as a genre piece. Using previously untranslated information from Messiaen's own description of the work in his *Traité*, close analysis of the music seeks to demystify some of the complex innovations he made to his musical language, especially in the areas of rhythm and orchestration. This Element pays special attention to the fragmentary and elusive program, which is explained with reference to Messiaen's fascination with surrealism at this time. Information is included on the commission and composition of the piece, its premiere by the Boston Symphony Orchestra conducted by Leonard Bernstein, its revision by Messiaen in 1990, and its reception history in both live and recorded performances.

Keywords: Messiaen, *Turangalîla-symphonie*, Tristan, Boston Symphony Orchestra, surrealism

ISBNs: 9781009165730 (PB), 9781009165723 (OC)
ISSNs: 2632-7791 (online), 2632-7783 (print)

Contents

My opinion is that this symphony is, after *Le sacre du printemps*, the greatest composition written in our century.

– Serge Koussevitzky[1]

1 Introduction

Messiaen's *Turangalîla-symphonie* is a vast and complex love song. Lasting around 85 minutes, and composed for enormous orchestral forces, this ten-movement symphonic masterpiece is a pioneering landmark in twentieth-century orchestral music by virtue of its innovations in orchestration, rhythm, melody, harmony, and form. Writing in 1995, just a few years after Messiaen's death in 1992, musicologist Malcolm Hayes noted that it is "beyond serious dispute" that "*Turangalîla* has attained the status of a classic," adding that the piece "must at the time have seemed gargantuan in its elaborate instrumental apparatus, hectic invention, flagrantly inflated rhetoric, and total lack of personal and artistic inhibition" (Hayes, 1995: 190). Since then, the piece has retained its place in the canon and has been regularly performed and recorded.

The symphony is important as part of Messiaen's oeuvre for several reasons. It marks the first significant expansion of his international career, and it solidified his reputation in the US (which led to his invitation to teach at the Boston Symphony Orchestra's summer home at Tanglewood). It is one of only a few pieces that does not have an explicit theological program but instead forms part of a trilogy of works based on the Tristan myth. While his personal faith and religious works in general have been widely discussed, the works of the Tristan Trilogy (*Harawi*, *Turangalîla-symphonie*, and *Cinq rechants*) have been discussed comparatively little, not least because the programmatic elements are fragmentary, highly personal, and not presented in the customary ways composers link music and meaning.

The piece is especially important in the development of Messiaen's musical technique and personal style. It contains numerous innovations, including the manipulation of themes and their meanings, its length, and its large performing forces (with solo piano, ondes Martenot, and a huge array of percussion). It is the closest he came to writing a piano concerto and is a significant work in his professional relationship with the pianist Yvonne Loriod (whose technical prowess undoubtedly influenced the piano writing). It is particularly notable for the development of several aspects of his unique rhythmic style. These are detailed in what follows and include additive rhythms; rhythmic cells; tâlas and superpositioned rhythms; rhythmic characters; and generative, periodic, progressive, and recursive rhythms.

---

[1] NBC interview with Olin Downes, broadcast November 28, 1949 (see Simeone, 2008: 41).

Olivier Messiaen was one of the most influential composers, teachers, and performers of the twentieth century, yet only within the last twenty years has he been afforded the same degree of scholarly attention as composers such as Schoenberg or Stravinsky. A flurry of publications after the centenary of the composer's birth in 2008 began to address compositional style and technique, theological themes, and general analysis of some prominent works. A major biography by Peter Hill and Nigel Simeone in 2005 presented a comprehensive insight into his life and, more recently (following the death of Yvonne Loriod), work has begun on his archives held at the Bibliothèque nationale de France. Several notable collections of essays (including *Messiaen Studies* [Sholl, 2007]) have expanded the scope of Messiaen scholarship, but there are very few books that cover repertoire (except for *Quatuor pour la fin du Temps*, which has received a lot of attention). Brief analysis and commentary on the symphony were provided in two survey collections published during Messiaen's lifetime (see Sherlaw Johnson, 1975 [especially 82–94]; and Griffiths, 1985 [especially 128–42]), and a short but informative essay in German by Klaus Schweizer appeared in 1982. Two books place the symphony in the context of the Tristan Trilogy and related works (Davidson, 2001; and Bruhn, 2008). In addition, there are many program notes that are largely based on Messiaen's own notes for the work. The principal scholarly work, however, is presented in theses and dissertations dating back to 1975. These include an analysis of the gamelan group (Bradbury, 1991), an algebraic study of rhythm (Hook, 1998), a study of pitch organization (Fancher, 2003), and an exploration of the cyclic themes (Byrne, 2009).

Messiaen wrote a great deal about his own music. In the early part of his career this led to "le cas Messiaen," a public debate which centered around criticisms of Messiaen's program notes, his theological aspirations, and his original style. Most of the information for specific works provided by Messiaen is in the form of written commentaries and in conversations he had with various journalists, critics, and scholars who engaged with him and his music in detail (see especially Goléa, 1961; and Samuel, 1967/1986). Despite "le cas Messiaen," this Element utilizes Messiaen's own descriptions of the *Turangalîla-symphonie* because they are concise and definitive statements about his intentions and vivid descriptions of the musical material. When analyzed, they reveal much about his compositional process, and many are presented here for the first time in English translation.[2]

This Element covers many aspects of the *Turangalîla-symphonie*. Section 2 provides information on the context, commission, and composition of the symphony along with information about the first performances by the Boston

---

[2] All translations are my own unless otherwise noted. Material from Messiaen's analysis in the second volume of his *Traité de rythme, de couleur, et d'ornithologie* is cited in the abbreviated form (*Traité*: page number).

Symphony Orchestra conducted by Leonard Bernstein. Using information provided by Messiaen in several sources, but especially from the second volume of his *Traité* (Messiaen, 1995), Section 3 provides an overview of the various programmatic elements of the Tristan found in the symphony. Section 4 provides a brief introduction to Messiaen's unique compositional style as a prelude to Section 5, which is dedicated to a detailed analysis of each movement. This analysis seeks to demystify some of the complex innovations he made to his musical language, especially in the areas of rhythm and orchestration. Section 6 discusses the changes made to the score in 1990 that provide further insight into his compositional process.[3] Section 7 discusses the reception history of the work in live and recorded performances along with ballet versions and some documentaries about the work. Finally, concluding remarks in Section 8 assess the piece, offer suggestions for understanding the program, and advocate for its continued place in the canon.

2 Context, Commission, Composition, and Premiere

Messiaen was born in 1908 and studied at the Paris Conservatoire. During his career as a composer Messiaen returned to the Paris Conservatoire to teach harmony and composition from 1941 until his retirement in 1978. He was also a church musician and held the titular post as organist of Sainte-Trinité Church in Paris from 1931 until his death in 1992.

The American composer Virgil Thomson, writing in the *New York Herald Tribune* on September 23, 1945 (some four years before the *Turangalîla* premiere), succinctly summarizes the prevailing opinion about the radical music of the young French composer:

> What strikes one right off on hearing any of his pieces is the power these have of commanding attention. They do not sound familiar; their textures – rhythmic, harmonic and instrumental – are fresh and strong. And though a certain melodic banality may put one off no less than the pretentious mysticism of his titles may offend, it is not possible to come in contact with any of his major productions without being aware that one is in the presence of a major musical talent. Liking it or not is of no matter: Messiaen's music has a vibrancy that anybody can be aware of, that the French music world is completely aware of, that has been accepted here indeed for the post-war period as take it or leave it, one of the facts of life.

While the charge of "pretentious mysticism" seems a little unfair given what we now know of Messiaen's devout Catholicism, it is true that some audiences still struggle with this aspect of the composer's work.

---

[3] The score has a copyright date of 1992 but was not published until June 1994 according to the dépôt legal copy in the Bibliothèque nationale.

Messiaen's reputation was initially based on some organ works and song cycles. Only four surviving orchestral works predate *Turangalîla*: *Les Offrandes oubliées* (1930), *Le Tombeau resplendissant* (1930), *Hymne au Saint-Sacrement* (1932), and *L'Ascension* (1932–3). In addition, Messiaen composed several works for orchestra and chorus. Some of these were entries for a composition prize, the prestigious Prix de Rome (which he never won), including *La Sainte-Bohème* (1930) and *La jeunesse des vieux* (1931). Hill and Simeone, 2005: 28, 31. In 1937, Messiaen arranged his own song cycle, *Poèmes pour Mi*, for orchestra, but it was his *Trois petites liturgies de la présence divine* (1944) for women's chorus and orchestra (with ondes Martenot) that helped to spread his reputation abroad. Messiaen learned about orchestration while a student, but he also studied (and taught) works by many canonic composers, including Debussy and Stravinsky. His orchestral writing was also influenced by his work as an organist and especially by the organ that Messiaen regularly played, made by the renowned Aristide Cavaillé-Coll in Sainte-Trinité. This orchestrally conceived instrument allowed Messiaen to experiment with different timbres, registers, and dynamics that resulted in highly original sounds not only for his organ works but also for his orchestral compositions.

The Commission and Composition

The Russian-born composer and conductor Serge Koussevitzky was an early champion of Messiaen's work, having conducted *Les Offrandes oubliées* (1930) in Boston with the Boston Symphony Orchestra during their 1936 season. This was the first ever performance of a work by Messiaen outside France (Simeone, 2008: 26). Koussevitzky's support continued and, in a letter dated June 25, 1945, he commissioned Messiaen to write something under the auspices of the Music Foundation, set up in memory of his second wife Natalie, who died in 1942. The fee was $1,000 and, other than requesting a dedication to the Koussevitzky Music Foundation and that the manuscript be given to the Foundation, no other specifics were mentioned (Ibid. 31). Messiaen was greatly honored by the commission, responding:

> I want to make every effort to write a work that will be beautiful and of significant proportions. To succeed, I need time to dream about it, to love it, to perfect it, and to orchestrate it without rushing. That will require a minimum of six months, a maximum of one year. I am going to think about all this now, and will keep you up to date with my work (Ibid.).

According to Messiaen, the piece was composed and orchestrated between July 17, 1946, and November 29, 1948 (*Traité*: 151). The order in which he composed the ten movements is interesting because it helps us to trace musical ideas in different movements and to see how the composition developed from a four-movement work to the ten-movement finished piece. Messiaen described the process: "I first wrote movements 1, 4, 6 and 10. Then the three rhythmic studies called 'Turangalîla' 1, 2, and 3. Then no. 2. Then the large development which is no. 8. And I finished with no. 5" (Hill and Simeone, 2005: 160). Biographers Peter Hill and Nigel Simeone suggest that "it is probable that he followed his custom of composing the work in short score, only then turning his attention to the orchestration" (Ibid.). Notes in Messiaen's diary at the end of 1947 give information concerning both a ten-movement and a nine-movement version of the work. In the ten-movement version, music for the "Finale" was used twice, but only once in the nine-movement version (Ibid.: 171):

Titles and subtitles for the *Symphonie-Tâla*

1. Introduction (old first movement)
2. 1st Tâla
3. Chant de rêve (old second movement)
4. 2nd Tâla
5. Sonata (old fifth movement)
6. Chant de tendresse (old fourth movement)
7. Chant de passion (old eighth movement)
8. 3rd Tâla
9. Kheyâla-Mâruta (old third movement)
10. Finale (use the old fifth movement again, in perpetual semiquavers by the whole orchestra *fff*)

or nine movements:

1. Introduction
2. Chant de rêve
3. 1st Tâla (with birdsongs on the piano)
4. Chant de tendresse
5. Kheyâla-Mâruta
6. 2nd Tâla
7. Chant de passion
8. 3rd Tâla (with ondes and clarinet only, using rhythmic series)
9. Finale (the old fifth movement orchestrated *fff*)
Order: *Bien.*

The following is the final order of the movements and an idea of their comparative length using timings from the 1991 Deutsche Grammophon recording:

1.	Introduction	6:25
2.	Chant d'amour (Love song) 1	8:14
3.	Turangalîla 1	5:26
4.	Chant d'amour 2	11:03
5.	Joie du sang des étoiles (Joy of the Blood of the Stars)	6:42
6.	Jardin du sommeil d'amour (Garden of Love's Sleep)	12:39
7.	Turangalîla 2	4:11
8.	Développement d'amour (Development of Love)	11:41
9.	Turangalîla 3	4:27
10.	Final	7:44

The Meaning of *Turangalîla*

The final order, probably established early in 1948, renames several movements and gives a new title for the whole piece. In the liner notes for the 1991 Deutsche Grammophon recording, Messiaen wrote the following about the final title (which he had stated elsewhere, notably in conversation with Antoine Goléa [Goléa, 1961: 83]):

> *Turangalîla* – pronounced "tour-ahn-gu-lee-lah", with the last two syllables accented and lengthened – is a word in Sanskrit. As with all words from ancient oriental languages, its meaning is very rich. "Lila" literally means play – but play in the sense of the divine action upon the cosmos, the play of creation, of destruction, of reconstruction, the play of life and death. "Lila" is also Love. "Turanga": this is time that runs, like a galloping horse; this is time that flows, like sand in an hourglass. "Turanga" is movement and rhythm. "Turangalila" therefore means all at once love song, hymn to joy, time, movement, rhythm, life and death (Messiaen, 1991: 1).

In the *Traité* he noted that some thought the word was a young woman's name.[4] Interestingly, the *Traité* text omits the rest of the description of the two individual words, noting only that he chose the word "for its euphonic qualities. Simply because it sounded well, it was pleasant to hear" (*Traité*: 151).

As well as describing *Turangalîla* as a love song, Messiaen described it as a "hymn to joy" and elaborated on what he meant by joy:

---

[4] This is not the case, but it did become the name, in the Americanized version Turanga Leela, of the female lead in the animated science fiction TV show *Futurama*.

Not the bourgeois and quietly euphoric joy of some honest seventeenth-century man, but such that one can conceive of it who has only glimpsed it in the midst of misfortune, that is to say a superhuman joy, overflowing, blinding and excessive. Love is presented there under the same aspect: it is the fatal, irresistible love, which transcends everything, which suppresses everything outside itself, such as it is symbolized by the potion of Tristan and Isolde (*Traité*, 151).

These notions of superhuman joy and utterly transcendent love are the principal themes of the work and are elaborated and colored by other brief references Messiaen makes. These are collated and discussed further in the following analysis.

The Meaning of *symphonie*

While Messiaen was explicit about the meaning of the word *Turangalîla*, he was less clear about the term *symphonie*, which had been part of the title since the early conception of the piece. It could be that he meant it in its literal meaning of "sounding together," however, *Turangalîla* does have some formal similarities with the symphonic genre: movements 4 and 5 could be likened to the scherzo (as Messiaen himself suggested), movement 8 is an extended development, movement 9 is a set of variations, and movement 10 is a modified sonata form. Other traditional techniques used in the symphony include cyclical themes, thematic development across movements, and an extramusical program.[5] Even though he named four themes, Messiaen avoided the term leitmotif because he felt it was too influenced by the way Wagner used it. Despite these traditional elements, the symphony includes many innovative techniques, which suggests that Messiaen was saying something new about the form.

The *Trois Tâla*

Scholars have traced the development of the three movements once collected as a group under the title *Trois Tâla*, which became movements 3, 4, and 5 of the symphony. The *Trois Tâla* were rehearsed (in front of an audience) as a set on February 14, 1948, and premiered the following day. They were conducted by André Cluytens with Yvonne Loriod and Ginette Martenot as soloists (for more, see Baeck, 2017: 153–179). Hill and Simeone believe these performances were simply a chance for Messiaen to hear the pieces live and evaluate whether or not they were successful. Baeck suggests "he first chose the title *Trois Tâla* in order to make possible the performance of three movements from a symphony commissioned by the Koussevitzky Foundation without attracting the attention of its sponsors before the world premiere" (Baeck, 2017: 168). It is clear, though, that

---

[5] For more on this, see McNeill, 2010.

Messiaen never intended them to be stand-alone works and they were never published, although they were performed again in Vienna on June 28, 1948, and on February 6, 1949, in Baden-Baden. Later, Messiaen was insistent that "The *Trois Tâla* never existed. Through the publisher Durand I forbade the improper use of this title ... I have never been of the view that my *Turangalîla* should be split into separate pieces. So this title should not be used, as it is misleading" (Hill and Simeone, 2005: 173).

Messiaen made contradictory remarks about whether selected movements of the symphony should be performed. In the preface to the first edition of the score, Messiaen notes that he conceived the symphony "as a whole" and that he therefore prefers the piece to be performed "complete and without interruption" (although the Boston premiere included an interval after movement 5). He also indicated that the length may be off-putting and that conductors may prefer to perform only parts of the work. He therefore provided some options for the performance of selected movements:

1. Movements 3 (Turangalîla 1), 4 (Song of love 2), and 5 (Joy of the blood of the stars).
2. The three Turangalîla movements in the order 7, 9, 3.
3. A "shortcut" version of the whole symphony in this order: 1 (Introduction), 6 (Garden of the sleep of love), 2 (Love song 1), 4 (Love song 2), 10 (Finale).

Messiaen advocated for the first option as the best, since it had already been performed this way many times. He also notes that because movement 8 is "the grand development of thematic elements of the work it absolutely cannot appear in a selection," but notes that movement 5 (Joy of the blood of the stars) can be performed alone since it is "sufficient in itself."

The *Trois Tâla* received reviews that Baeck characterizes as "rather mixed in Paris (where the traditionalist opinions of the critics and the public prevailed), downright negative in Vienna (the capital of the old empire Austro-Hungarian still suffering after the war from cultural isolation due to the Anschluss and the disaster of the war), but more positive, if not enthusiastic in Baden-Baden" (Baeck, 2017: 169). The critic for the *Wiener Kurier* pointed to one of the most problematic issues for Messiaen's music, namely how much of what is going on beyond the audible surface of the music should be comprehended by the listener. The critic follows Messiaen's program note for the Vienna performance (slightly longer than the one for the Paris premiere) and notes that Messiaen set out to compose "a love song in three parts (sad – tender – passionate);" however, the critic also observes that for the audience, this "cannot even be discerned with the sensitivity of a seismograph without the author's explanations in the program" (Baeck, 2017: 161). This perennial issue for Messiaen's music is discussed further in what follows.

Baeck quotes the brief program note Messiaen provided for the performance of the *Trois Tâla* in Vienna on June 28, 1948, which provides some interesting background about the form and content of the three *Turangalîla* movements (Baeck, 2017: 160). Messiaen first asserts that "the work is a love song," a comment he repeatedly made about all three of the Tristan works, but of *Turangalîla* in particular. He then goes on to describe the importance of rhythm for the three pieces and ascribes to them certain emotional characteristics:

> Tâla is a word in the Hindu language which means rhythm. The three pieces are an essay on rhythmic language. The rhythms, which are based on many entirely new principles (values of quantity, dynamic values, alternation between arsis and thesis, added values, non-retrogradability) are used to express a violent love: sad in the first Tâla, tender in the second, violently passionate in the third.

The description Messiaen provided of the form and content of each movement offers useful clues to the *Turangalîla* movements and is similar to his later commentaries:

> 1st Tâla: A nostalgic theme played on the ondes Martenot. Followed by a heavier theme on the trombones. A slow vocalise on the oboe. The vibraphone and the glockenspiel produce sounds resembling a gamelan. Four rhythmic forms are used: rhythmic decrease in zigzag, rhythmic increase in scissor form [i.e., fan form in which music plays forwards and backwards like the opening or closing of a fan; see *Traité* 3: 325], retrograde rhythmic canon and rhythm with asymmetrical enlargement with three rhythmic characters on maracas, wood block, and bass drum.
>
> 2nd Tâla: Scherzo theme exhibited by the piccolo, the bassoon and decreased [*réduire*] on the piano. After the bridge Trio 1 follows on the winds: a love song of great depth; undulating rhythms and voluptuous choice of durations. Trio 2 is also a love song, played with more flexibility on the strings. Bird songs on piano and vibraphone that mingle with the superposition of the two Trios. After another bridge, superposition of the Scherzo and the two Trios. Piano cadenza. Coda on the love song, even more tender and more sweet.
>
> 3rd Tâla: Long dance of love and joy; the full orchestra is unleashed, violently swirling with passion. Alternation between chorus and verses in the dance of love. First development, very passionate, [with] rhythms in three pronounced characters in asymmetrical enlargement, borrowed from the love dance (brass). Resumption of the chorus in the distance. Resumption of development simultaneously backwards and forwards: the result is a rhythmically retrograde canon of the three rhythmic characters with trumpets and trombones. Resumption of the chorus in the distance, an ostinato bass on the chorus variation. The coda develops in a manner more and more dynamic up to the maximum height of strength and passion. Piano cadenza and brass increase to the climax (Ibid.).

This analysis is developed further in Section 5, but for now let us return to the chronology of the symphony.

The Premiere and Initial Reception

The *Turangalîla* premiere was given in Boston's Symphony Hall on December 2, 1949, by the Boston Symphony Orchestra conducted by Leonard Bernstein with Yvonne Loriod (piano), and Ginette Martenot (ondes Martenot). It was reprised by the same performers on December 3 in Boston and on December 10 at Carnegie Hall in New York. The French premiere took place on July 25, 1950, at the Festival International d'Aix-en-Provence by the Orchestre National de la RTF conducted by Roger Désormière.

For the Boston premiere, the work was allotted ten rehearsals, a comparatively generous amount of time, but necessary given the complexity of the work. A twenty-six-minute recording of a rehearsal was released as part of a boxed set entitled "Leonard Bernstein: Historic Broadcasts, 1946–1961" by West Hill Radio Archives in 2013. It begins with part of the NBC interview with Koussevitzky that was broadcast prior to the premiere in which he invites patience from the public, describing the symphony as "new in every way." The rehearsal concentrates primarily on the fifth and sixth movements but actually contains very little of Bernstein's direction and nothing from Messiaen himself.[6]

In general, the premiere was not well received. Critic Cyrus Durgin, writing in the *Boston Globe* on December 3, 1949, praises the orchestra but echoes the audience reaction and is unimpressed with the music:

> "*Turangalîla*" is a girl's name, and a poetic Indian word for love song, and it is also the title of a gigantic and ear-blasting new Symphony by Olivier Messiaen ... As music it isn't much, but it has focused attention upon the subject of love in the East Indies, and that is something even in Boston. ...
> Upon reading [the titles of the individual movements] in the program book I was at once convinced they were inflammatory and searched for a nickel to call up the censor. But when the music began, it was quickly evident how wrong one can be. ... At intermission the lobbies buzzed with rebellious and treasonous objections, and by the time the second half began a good many of the Friday afternoon subscribers had departed. ...
> The real heroes were Mr. Bernstein and the gentlemen of the orchestra, for they must have put in many hours of exhausting effort with this tricky and futile work (Simeone, 2002: 114).

After the French premiere in 1950, composer Francis Poulenc described the work as "atrocious," "dishonest," and "written to please both the crowd and

---

[6] A link to the BSO rehearsal with Bernstein and other audio visual links can be found at www.cambridge.org/Shenton.

the élite, the bidet and the baptismal font, all in the awful tradition of Dukas and Marcel Dupré" (Hill and Simeone, 2005: 195). In order to understand the audience reaction it is important to appreciate just how unusual and unique Messiaen's style was and how he developed traditional techniques to new ends.

3 Messiaen's Musical Style

Messiaen sounds like Messiaen. Few composers adopted or adapted his style, even though he taught many prominent composers at the Conservatoire (although there is no doubt his innovations have directly influenced many subsequent composers). Even the early works sound strikingly original, and his technique developed so fast he felt it necessary to publish a brief introduction to his innovative compositional methods in the preface to his nine-movement organ cycle *La Nativité du Seigneur* (Messiaen, 1935) that describes five principal means of musical expression: modes, pedal appoggiaturas, added values, gradually increasing intervals, and the chord on the dominant (which contains all the notes of the major scale).[7] Further details of his musical language were described in the preface to the score of the *Quatuor pour la fin du Temps* (Messiaen, 1942), and this was quickly followed by a detailed musical treatise titled *Technique de mon langage musical*, which was published in two volumes (one of text and one of musical examples) in 1944.[8] Messiaen taught at the Paris Conservatoire from 1941 to 1978 and collected his teaching and other writings into his *Traité de rythme, de couleur, et d'ornithologie* published posthumously in seven tomes (tome 5 is published in two separate books). Messiaen continued to describe elements of his compositional technique in the liner and program notes for various pieces. For the 1991 Deutsche Grammophon recording, for example, he includes detailed discussion of several innovations in *Turangalîla*, including two rhythmic features (rhythmic characters, and nonretrogradable rhythms), as well as the unusual orchestration of the work.

Messiaen developed his style continuously, notably contributing to total serialism, a development from Schoenberg's twelve-tone system that applied the notion of serial choice to other principal musical features including dynamics and types of attack. This first appeared in "Mode de valeurs et d'intensités," the second of his *Quatre études de rythme* (1949–50). Also interesting, but far less influential than his serial technique developments, is his "langage communicable," a sophisticated mapping of written language to music using a musical

---

[7] For a general introduction to Messiaen's musical technique, see Pople, 1995.

[8] This was published in John Satterfield's English translation in 1956 and republished as a single volume in 1999.

alphabet and a system of leitmotifs, developed for the organ cycle *Méditations sur le mystère de la Sainte Trinité* (1967–9), but also used briefly in passages in *Des canyons aux étoiles . . .* (1971–4) and the *Livre du Saint Sacrement* (1984).

In order to grasp the compositional developments in the symphony it is important to understand the idiosyncratic and individual elements of his musical language, which can be summarized under five headings.

Faith and Love

Messiaen's Catholic devotion pervades his life and work. Almost all of his music has an explicitly religious program, and he wrote detailed notes describing how the religious content is portrayed in the music. He stated: "The illumination of the theological truths of the Catholic faith is the first aspect of my work, the noblest, and no doubt the most useful and most valuable – perhaps the only one I won't regret at the hour of my death" (Samuel, 1994: 20). He also admitted that "I am a human being, and like all others I am susceptible to human love, which I expressed in three of my works that incorporate the greatest myth of human love, that of Tristan and Isolde" (Ibid.).

Birdsong

Messiaen developed his *style oiseau* by altering bird songs, transcribing them in a slower tempo, lowering their register, and removing microtones while maintaining integrity in the intervallic structure of each song (see Samuel, 1994: 95). In his early works, Messiaen's use of birdsong is limited and rather vague. In the *Quatuor pour la fin du Temps*, for example, he describes certain musical lines as "comme un oiseau"; however, during the 1950s birdsong dominates his music and includes specific and detailed birdsong, often developed at length. His *Catalogue d'oiseaux* (1956–8) is devoted to the music of birds. It contains thirteen pieces, which are named after birds in different regions in France. The importance of birds as a source of inspiration is also signaled by the fact that Messiaen devoted the fifth volume of his *Traité* entirely to his use of birdsong, providing 655 pages of text and examples in two volumes.[9]

Modes of Limited Transposition and Harmony

These are scales with limited capability for transposition before returning to pitches of the mode in a different order. As Messiaen explains, "these modes are formed of several symmetrical groups, the last note of each group always being common with the first of the following group. At the end of a certain number of

---

[9] For more on Messiaen's use of birdsong, see Fallon, 2007; and Kraft, 2013.

chromatic transpositions which varies with each mode, they are no longer transposable, giving exactly the same notes as the first" (Messiaen, 1944: 58). Messiaen uses seven modes. Other modes exist; however, they are truncations of the original seven.

Example 1 Mode 3
www.cambridge.org/Shenton

Mode 3 is divided into three groups of four notes each (see Example 1). It contains the intervals tone, semitone, semitone, tone, semitone, semitone, tone, semitone, semitone, and has four transpositions. Messiaen uses these modes for harmonic as well as melodic material. He also uses the harmonic series to build "special chords" (*accords speciaux*), such as the chords of contracted resonance and the color chords.[10]

Rhythm

By the mid-1940s Messiaen had already developed a signature approach to rhythms that included many different approaches to their creation and manipulation. These include:

- nonretrogradable (palindromic) rhythms
- additive values (the addition of a dot or rest to a rhythm without the confines of strict time signatures)
- Greek rhythms (poetic forms)
- Hindu rhythms (deći-tâlas, found in the book *Samgîta-ratnâkara* written by the thirteenth-century Indian musicologist Çârngadeva [1175–1247])
- symmetrical permutations (also called interversions), which are the swapping of the positions of rhythms within a sequence
- chromatic durations (in which sequences of rhythms are extended or shortened by defined parameters)

The importance of rhythm as a compositional technique is underscored by its prominent place in his *Traité*. The first volume begins with a discussion of the philosophical and scientific notions of time and includes information on Greek metric patterns and the Indian rhythmic patterns that he utilized as the basis for various rhythmic formulations of his own. Volume 2 of the *Traité* expands on his specific techniques of nonretrogradable rhythms, rhythmic pedals and canons, rhythmic characters, and irrational values. *Traité* 2 also includes

---

[10] For more on Messiaen's chords, see Cheong Wai-Ling, 2003.

detailed discussion of symmetry using examples from nature (butterfly wings), architecture, language (palindromes), and numerology.

In the program for the premiere of *Turangalîla*, Messiaen wrote that the piece

> is written in a very special rhythmic language and makes use of several new rhythmic principles (quantitative [note values], dynamic [intensity], cinematic [movement], phonetic [timbre], added values, non-reversible rhythms, asymmetric augmentations with several rhythmic characters [*personnages rhythmiques*], rhythmic modes, and the combination of quantitative and sounding elements in reinforcing the values and the timbre of each percussion instrument by chords which form the resonance [overtones] of these timbres (Messiaen, 1949b: 352).

The rhythmic characters are an interesting technique for musical development. Messiaen described them as

> certain groups of rhythmic values that each lead their own life. I use them often, these rhythmic characters, and I vary them according to different processes: one variant increases the fundamental form, another decreases, a third alternates between increase and decrease, a fourth remains unchanged. It makes you think of different characters on a stage: one acts, the other assists as a spectator, the two are adversaries, we separate, we shout, etc. (Baeck, 2017: 175).

As shown in the analyses that follow, *Turangalîla* extends these ideas to great complexities, especially when they are combined with Messiaen's other rhythmic techniques.[11]

Color

Messiaen had a type of synesthesia whereby sounds would invoke specific colors, often in great detail.[12] For him, each musical mode has specific colors associated with each of their different transpositions. Mode 2 in first transposition, for example, he describes as "blue-violet rocks speckled with little gray cubes, cobalt blue, deep Prussian blue, highlighted by a bit of violet-purple, gold, red, ruby, and stars of mauve, black, and white. Blue-violet is dominant!" (Samuel, 1986: 64). Messiaen believed that "There aren't any modal composers, tonal composers or serial composers. There is only music that is colored and music that isn't" (Ibid.: 63).

---

[11] For more detail on rhythmic characters, see *Traité* 2, section III, p. 91. This volume of the *Traité* also includes detailed descriptions of nonretrogradable rhythms, augmentations and diminutions, and pedals and rhythmic canons.

[12] See *Traité* 7 and Bernard, 1986.

Orchestration

Although for Messiaen color may be conjured up by scales and pitches regardless of timbre, for most people listening to his music it is the orchestration that provides much of the music's color. In keeping with Messiaen's note to Koussevitzky that the piece would be "of significant proportions," Messiaen scored *Turangalîla* for large orchestra, the largest he had written for to date. The instrumentation for the woodwind, brass, and strings is as follows:

> Woodwind: piccolo, two flutes, two oboes, cor anglais, two clarinets, bass clarinet (all three in B-flat and in A), three bassoons
> Brass: four horns in F, three trumpets, trumpet in D, cornet, three trombones, tuba
> Strings: 32 violins (16 first, 16 second), 14 violas, 12 cellos, 10 double basses

There is nothing particularly unusual about the instruments of these sections; however, Messiaen also uses many keyboard and percussion instruments. The percussion instruments are played by five people, and Messiaen notes in the preface to the score which player covers which instruments for each movement. The instruments are triangle, three temple blocks, wood block, small Turkish cymbal, three cymbals (one suspended), Chinese cymbal, tam-tam, tambourine, maracas, Provencal drum, snare drum, bass drum, and eight tubular bells. Since he has this large array of pitches and timbres, he dispenses with the timpani commonly found in symphonic orchestrations. Messiaen characterizes the percussion both by pitch and timbre and notes the difficulty of the music he wrote for them, insisting that the piece needs first-rate percussionists who have a sixth sense about playing precisely, and that any small errors could destroy the music (*Traité*: 156).

The Gamelan Group

Messiaen ascribed a particular role to a group of keyboard instruments (glockenspiel, celesta, and vibraphone united with the piano and metallic percussion) that he described as "similar to that of an East Indian gamelan, as used in the islands of the Sonde (such as Java and Bali)" (Messiaen, 1949b: 348). In the *Traité* Messiaen describes how he first heard a gamelan ensemble at the 1931 World's Fair in Paris and how the rhythms and timbres of the Legong dance left an indelible impression on him. How this relates to the program of the symphony is not clear; however, it is likely that Messiaen used the group as an orchestral character (similar to his use of rhythmic and harmonic characters), and that this group acts in certain ways in counterpart to the other orchestral groupings.

The Piano

In addition to being part of the gamelan group, there is an extensive part for solo piano of such prominence and difficulty that Messiaen stated that *Turangalîla* is "almost a concerto for piano and orchestra," and noted that "long and brilliant cadenzas form parts of the various movements, binding the elements of development together, constituting an integral part of the form" (Messiaen, 1953/ 1994, 155). He avoided the term concerto for the title perhaps because there is also a notably virtuosic part for the ondes Martenot, but also perhaps because it is an ensemble piece with virtuosic parts for many players. It is also difficult to attach the vague and surreal program to the historical connotations of the term concerto, even if one were to try to establish a connection between the two principal solo instruments and the two principal characters of Tristan and Isolde.

The technical difficulty of the piano part is influenced by the prodigious technique of Yvonne Loriod (1924–2010), who had premiered the *Vingt Regards sur l'Enfant-Jésus* (1944) and (with Messiaen) the *Visions de l'Amen* (1943). Loriod and Messiaen married in 1961 following the death of his first wife, Claire Delbos, in 1959. In the introduction to his analysis in the *Traité*, Messiaen describes some of the piano techniques that enrich the ensemble, including complex birdsongs, arpeggios, and cascades of chords. He also gives specific examples of where the piano has a very specific role in the music, such as throughout the sixth movement (Jardin du sommeil d'amour) where it "embroiders a counterpoint of birdsong above the love theme," or in the fifth and tenth movements where the piano adds to the dynamism of the orchestra as it unleashes its own dynamism (*Traité*: 155).

The Ondes Martenot

It isn't often that new instruments are created, but the advent of electricity and the discovery of ways to use it to produce musical sounds resulted in some instruments that attempted to recreate an existing instrument such as the valve organ, and others, such as the theremin, that were entirely new in their sound output. The ondes was created by Maurice Martenot in 1928 and can be played in a variety of different ways, depending on the model. Messiaen may have become acquainted with the instrument through Jeanne Loriod, sister of Yvonne Loriod. Jeanne and Yvonne performed together in many subsequent renditions of the piece; however, for the premiere, Ginette Martenot, the sister of the instrument's inventor, was the soloist.

Figure 1 An Ondes Martenot

In the *Traité* Messiaen explains briefly how the instrument works and then provides detail about the specific timbres that are available, noting that the instrument can be extremely quiet but also so loud that it is almost painful for the listener. Because the ondes is capable of playing so many different sounds, Messiaen explains how he wants the instrument configured and played using the conventional notation suggested by Martenot himself. The first use of the instrument in movement 1, for example, has the indication "Ruban-métalisé amplifié-M 4321" (Score: 3), which indicates use of the ribbon rather than the keyboard, with the metalized diffuser, followed by a series of numbers representing buttons on the instrument, which reinforce or reduce the number of harmonics in use.

Messiaen's comments indicate that against the backdrop of a large but traditional symphonic ensemble he has placed two solo instruments and a range of percussion that have defined roles in presenting both musical and extramusical material. Before delving into analysis of the individual movements, it is important to understand the elements of Messiaen's program for the piece and how these can be understood by the listener.

4 The Tristan Trilogy and the Extramusical Program

In his own analysis of the symphony, Messiaen is quick to point to it being part of a trilogy of works composed between 1945 and 1948, and that to understand

Turangalîla it is important to recognize that it is framed by the song cycle *Harawi* (for dramatic soprano and piano, 1945), and *Cinq rechants* (for 12 mixed voices, 1948). All three use the legend of Tristan and Isolde for subject material, but in very different ways (*Traité*: 150). These works are unusual in Messiaen's output, since they concentrate on human rather than divine love. This was Messiaen's preoccupation for several years, since the only other works composed during this time were *Chant des déportés* (1945), a commission from Radio France honoring the liberation of prisoners from German concentration camps; and *Cantéyodjayâi* (for piano, 1948), a work that belongs more to the experimental works of the late forties and early fifties such as the *Quatre études de rythme* (for piano, 1949–50). For Messiaen, *Harawi*, *Turangalîla*, and the *Cinq rechants* are "three aspects – of instrumental material, intensity, import-ance and style – of one and the same Tristan" (*Traité*: 151).

Messiaen the Surrealist

In an interview in 1953, Messiaen declared, "I am not a mystical musician, but a Surrealist musician who exceeds his desire for the Surreal by the supernatural" (Guth, 1953: 4). During sessions for the 1961 Véga recording of *Turangalîla*, he remarked that his music for the Tristan Trilogy period was "more or less surrealist," and his texts and commentaries attempted to emulate the style of two prominent contributors to the movement, André Breton and Paul Éluard (both of whom are mentioned in Messiaen's notes about *Turangalîla*).[13] Breton's *Manifeste du surréalisme* of 1924 defined the movement as one that "is the dictation of thought, free from any control by reason and of any aesthetic or moral preoccupation," but it is his definition in his *Second Manifeste du surréalisme* of 1930 that more succinctly summarizes the ideas Messiaen presents in the trilogy. Breton suggests that surrealists were aiming for "a mental vantage-point from which life and death, the real and the imaginary, past and future, communicable and incommunicable, high and low, will no longer be conceived as contradictions" (*Britannica*, and Hill and Simeone, 2005: 168). In a conversation published in *Revue musicale de France* in 1946, interviewer Ernest de Gengenbach notes that previously there had been no surrealist composers, but suggests that Messiaen's music could be considered surrealist music "because it draws its inspiration from elements of the fantastic in Christianity to which access is granted thanks to the loving prayer of a soul who resonates, like a harp, under the fingers of the Artist, of the Poet par excellence; of the Word, Creator of sound, of word, of colours" (Ibid.: 167). Gengenbach elides surrealism and Christianity in ways that Breton and others had not intended;

---

[13] For more on Messiaen's surrealism in *Harawi*, see Sholl, 2007; and on surrealism in his poetry, see Peterson, 1998.

however, his idea that Messiaen was around that time a surrealist composer is true. Surrealism aimed to blur the distinction between dream and reality and, as noted in Breton's manifestos, to free the creator from reason, obligation, and contradiction. Aspects of this can be seen in both *Harawi* and *Cinq rechants* by virtue of their texts; however, *Turangalîla* is textless, and Messiaen provided only clues as to how the program and music match.

Harawi

Harawi (subtitled "Songs of love and death") is a song cycle in 12 movements, lasting around 50 minutes, for which Messiaen wrote the surrealist text. It is a Peruvian version of the Tristan story, in which Isolde is named Piroutcha. Messiaen notes that his work is related "by text and melodic turn" to the musical genre known as Yaravi (in Spanish) or Harawi (in Quechua, the indigenous Peruvian language), a type of nostalgic love song.

In his analysis of *Harawi* in the third volume of the *Traité*, Messiaen's own description of the musical language is interesting. He notes that it includes much rhythmic innovation ("added values, non-retrogradable rhythms, rhythmic canons, 'irrational' values and short notes linked to longer ones, inexact augmentations, rhythmic characters, etc."); along with "non-classifiable chords and sonorities (notably the chords of inferior contracted resonance)," and "the pursuit of a melodic line that is vocal, simple, singing, with its own melodic cadences; birdsong; counterpoints of water drops; [and] atmospheric vibrations." The most important point, however, is that "It is finally, *and this is the only thing of import, a great cry of love*" [Messiaen's italics] (Messiaen, 1996: 282).

Cinq rechants

Messiaen believed *Cinq rechants* was one of his best works and noted he was fond of it (Samuel, 1994: 129). The work is in five movements lasting around 20 minutes. The musical sources of the *Cinq rechants* are diverse and include many Hindu rhythms, the verse/chorus style of the French renaissance composer Claude Le Jeune (which inspired the title), and the alba (poetry) of the troubadours. The text by Messiaen was "written partly in French, but mainly in a new language sometimes resembling Sanskrit and sometimes Quechua. It ultimately amounts to words invented by reason of their phonetic qualities, words whose vowels and consonants are arbitrarily chosen to correspond to certain rhythms and registers of the voice" (*Traité*: 151). The movements do not have titles but are usually noted using the first line of text. Here the untranslatable new language is omitted and only the first line of French indicated:

1. Les amoureux s'envolent (The lovers flee)
2. Ma première fois terre terre l'éventail déployé (My first time earth earth the fan unfolded)
3. Ma robe d'amour mon amour ma prison d'amour (My dress of love my love my prison of love)
4. Mon bouquet tout défait rayonne (My undone bouquet shines)
5. Tes yeux voyagent dans le passé (Your eyes wander into the past)

In the preface to the score Messiaen provides three performance instructions and a brief description of the language of the text and how to pronounce it. He asserts that "this work is a love song. This single word [love] is enough to guide the singers in the interpretation of the poem and the music."

In both *Harawi* and *Cinq rechants* there are words and phrases which Messiaen believed explain the themes of *Turangalîla* and which he set out in the *Traité* (p. 151). The movements that contain the quotes are noted in parentheses in the following list, as are any additional explanations by Messiaen. In *Harawi*:

> "Farewell to you, new light, / two-voiced potion." (7)
> "Enchained star, / Shared shadow, / In my hand my fruit of heaven, or day, / Distant love." (2 [first two lines] and 7 [all four lines])
> "All the birds of the stars." (10)
> "Shortest path from shadow to heaven." (10)
> "My love, my breath!" (12)
> "Let us invent the love of the world, / To seek each other / To cry for us, / To dream about us, / To find us." (12)

In *Cinq rechants*:

> "My dress of love, my love, / My prison of love, made of light air. / Lîla, lîla, my memory,
> / My caress ... " (3). (The air prison is an allusion to story of Merlin and Viviane.)
> "Lovers fly away; / Brangien, in space you are suffering ... " (1). (The lovers fly away, as in the paintings of Marc Chagall – and it's Brangien, the faithful Brangien who blows on them. Recall Brangäne's sublime calls during the love duet of *Tristan and Isolde* by Richard Wagner. These calls are a holdover from the old "Alba," where a friendly voice announced the return of dawn to lovers after a night of delights.)
> "Your eyes travel ... in the past ... in the future ... " (5). (We remember that the beautiful Isolde was a magician, skilled in potions, like her mother, and that, by her mysterious knowledge, she had saved Tristan from death, after he had been wounded by Morholt.)

Because these are surrealist texts it isn't possible to assemble them into narrative form, or perhaps even to understand them since they are so personal; however, they make more sense when we understand some of the other principal references and allusions in *Turangalîla*.

Programmatic Elements in *Turangalîla*

The idea of linking music to an extramusical program has been around for many centuries. Beethoven's sixth "Pastoral" symphony (1808), for example, has movement titles and includes musical depictions such as country dances, birdsongs, and a storm. Berlioz used literary works as inspiration for pieces such as his *Symphonie fantastique* (1830), and Liszt is credited with having invented the symphonic poem, a single movement form that represents and interprets a literary work (such as the *Dante Symphony* [1857] based on Dante's *Divine Comedy*). Because of his Christian faith, Messiaen's music is often packed with musical symbolism of various types, and his commentaries frequently tie pieces to theological ideas with varying degrees of specificity.

It is important to note that even though the Tristan myth is notably at the forefront of Messiaen's descriptions of his trilogy, divine love is also present. In an article titled "Querelle de la musique et de l'amour," which appeared in the French journal *Volontés* on May 16, 1945, Messiaen described how divine love is the creator of love in all its forms:

> There is so much that is dry and inhuman in contemporary music! Will our innovator be revolutionary only in his language? It seems almost certain that he will also bring new love. And not these blocks of despair, these uninhabited planets, but Love with a capital L, Love in all its forms: of Nature, of Woman, of Childhood, and above all Divine Love ... pray with me to the years, the days and the minutes that they may make haste to bring before us that innovator, that liberator who is so patiently awaited: the composer of Love (Quoted in Hill and Simeone, 2005: 153).

Turangalîla-symphonie, however, is specifically about "fatal, irresistible love," according to Messiaen himself, "which transcends everything outside itself, a love such as that symbolized by the love potion of Tristan and Isolde" (*Traité*: 151).

For *Turangalîla* the program is not explicit. It is not noted in the score, only in Messiaen's conversations, commentaries, and analysis. The program is not a linear narrative that follows the sequence of movements; instead, a series of vague hints and references are given. The program is comprised of episodic passages that Messiaen relates to specific musical strategies. As a prelude to the musical and thematic analysis described in what follows, this section collates and explains the primary literary and visual allusions Messiaen makes in the music, which helps to explain the specific programmatic elements that occur in the description of the work that follows. These allusions can be divided into three groups: A – myths and symbols of love, B – literary sources, and C – visual sources.[14]

A – Myths and Symbols of Love

1. The legend of Tristan and Isolde

Tristan and Isolde (or Iseult, or Yseult) is a medieval tragic love story which exists in many versions. The following are the salient elements for the symphony:

> Tristan ventures to Ireland to ask for the hand in marriage of the princess Isolde for his uncle, King Mark of Cornwall, and, having slain a dragon that is devastating the country, succeeds in his mission. On the homeward journey Tristan and Isolde drink a love potion prepared by the queen for her daughter and King Mark. Henceforth, the two are bound to each other by an imperishable love. King Mark tries to entrap the lovers; however, they flee into the forest of Morois. Tristan and Isolde make peace with Mark, and Tristan marries another woman also named Isolde. Tristan is wounded by a poisoned weapon and sends for the first Isolde who he believes could heal him. His wife tricks him into thinking she has not come, and he dies. When Isolde does arrive, she realizes she is too late to save him and dies in a final embrace. After their deaths two trees grow out of their graves and intertwine their branches so that they cannot be parted.

In his description of the story and the quotations he uses in his *Traité* analysis Messiaen refers to the version of the story as retold by Joseph Bédier, a professor at the Collège de France, in *Le Roman de Tristan et Iseult* published in 1900. Messiaen elaborates on aspects of the story that interested him, for example, the scene in the forest, which was filled with birdsong:

> The songs of birds abound in *Harawi* and in the "Jardin du sommeil d'amour" of *Turangalîla*. And I read in Bédier's admirable compilation and renewal: "But when the weather was clear, they erected their hut of green branches under the tall trees. Tristan knew from childhood the art of imitating the song of the woodland birds; at will, he imitated the oriole, the chickadee, the nightingale and all the winged birds; and, sometimes, on the branches of the hut, came to his call, many birds, swollen necks, sang their lays [lais] in the light. (*Roman de Tristan et Iseult* by Joseph Bédier – chapter IX, The forest of Morois) (*Traité*: 152).

---

[14] Information in the sections that follow was drawn from articles in *Encyclopedia Britannica* and *Britannica Academic*.

In conversation with Claude Samuel, Messiaen revealed that his version of Tristan actually has little to do with the Celtic legend: "I've preserved only the idea of a fatal and irresistible love, which, as a rule, leads to death and which, to some extent invokes death, for it is a love that transcends the body, transcends even the limitations of the mind, and grows to a cosmic scale" (Samuel, 1994: 30). This transcendent love falls into a hierarchy of love that Messiaen described to Samuel: "We start with trivial love ... before attaining the great human love, that magnificent love which is fatal passion. Then we reach maternal love, but divine love is at the top of the pyramid" (Ibid.: 31). In several places in his analysis, Messiaen focuses in on the aspect of human love that is at the heart of the trilogy, quoting, for example, a passage from Bédier that describes the all-consuming passion the lovers have for one another to the exclusion of all else, citing Tristan saying to Isolde: "If all the world were visible to us at once, I would see nothing but you" (*Traité*: 235).

The preoccupation of the trilogy is clearly with ecstatic and complete human love; however, Messiaen believed that "the nostalgia, the fatality of *Harawi*, the mysterious tenderness of the *Rechants*, are exceeded: *Turangalîla* is a hymn to Joy. The supraterrestrial joy of the unique and immortal love which is a reflection of the other Love" [i.e. divine love] (*Traité*: 153). For Messiaen, this joy is the result of intense love where two become one: "It's like a jump into infinity. There is no longer just a man and just a woman, but only one exceptional creature, whose halves want to join together," the result of which is that they attain "total and final astonishing happiness" (Ibid.). It is in support of this idea of cosmic love that Messiaen invoked similar circumstances in the love stories that follow.

2. Orpheus and Eurydice

Part of Greek mythology, Orpheus has superhuman musical ability, especially in singing and playing a lyre given to him by Apollo (in some versions). His wife Eurydice dies from a snakebite, and Orpheus travels to the underworld to rescue her by charming characters there, including Hades. She disappears, however, when he looks back to check whether she is still there. For Messiaen, this myth represents the strength of human emotion that compels Orpheus to descend into hell to free the woman he loves. In this myth the ending is tragic since he loses Eurydice forever. Messiaen was less interested in this part of the story than the strength of the love that Orpheus felt. Messiaen doesn't insist on us accepting all the symbolic content of the story but remarks, "I only notice that Orpheus was another musician" (*Traité*: 152). A specific reference to Orpheus occurs in movement 8, where Messiaen equates his music with the "nameless horrors" described in Edgar Allan Poe's short story *The Pit and the*

Pendulum, and describes how Orpheus and the lover of the Vénus d'Ille have found their true love in death (*Traité*: 331).

3. Bluebeard

The Bluebeard story is another one that has many versions. Messiaen would certainly have been familiar with the opera version by Paul Dukas (1907), based on the play *Ariande et Barbe-bleue* (1901) by Maurice Maeterlinck. Bluebeard is known for murdering each of his wives when they inquire about a forbidden room – the room where the previous wives' bodies are hanging. Messiaen traces the lineage to Gilles de Rais, or the Breton King Comor, but for him the origin of the story is not important. He describes what is important for *Turangalîla*: "Here is a key, a door, and a dark dungeon, a very dark little room full of terrible things that it is forbidden for us to know. And we are taught that the key is enchanted, and that once the door is opened, the irreparable is accomplished." Messiaen draws a parallel with the fatal moment the door is opened to the moment when Tristan and Isolde drink the love potion and are forever entwined, but states that "the symbol of Bluebeard is even more maddening!" without clarifying why this is the case (*Traité*: 152).

4. Medusa on Perseus's arm

The son of Zeus in Greek mythology, Perseus is known for decapitating Medusa the Gorgon. Perseus fell in love with the Ethiopian princess Andromeda and rescued her from a sea monster by showing it Medusa's head, which turned the sea monster into stone. For Messiaen, the importance of this story is that "The head of Medusa at the end of Perseus' arm assures him the most atrocious of victories" (Ibid.). The myth is only mentioned by Messiaen in his introduction to his own analysis, so it is not clear whether there are any direct correspondences in the music.

5. Vivien and Merlin

The legend of Merlin and Vivien appears in a three-volume version of the story titled *Les Chevaliers de la Table Ronde* by Jacques Boulenger (to which Messiaen refers), as well as other versions such as Tennyson's *Idylls of the King* (1859–85). Vivien is the paramour of King Mark of Cornwall. Sent to Camelot on a mission, Vivien convinces the magician Merlin to teach her a spell by claiming she is in love with him. Though he resists, he eventually gives in, and she uses the spell to imprison him in an invisible tower. What interests Messiaen in this story is not the suffering of Merlin who is imprisoned forever, but the strength of love Vivien has for Merlin that compels her actions. In conversation with Samuel, Messiaen describes this as "a greater and purer love" (Samuel, 1994: 31), and refers to the story in movements 6 and 8 of the symphony (*Traité*: 275, 312).

6. Pelléas and Mélisande

This story recounts Pelléas's tragic love for his half-brother Golaud's wife Mélisande. Messiaen knew the story from the symbolist play by Maeterlinck (1893), which Debussy used for an opera of the same name in 1902, and which was also used by composers such as Fauré and Schoenberg. As an homage, Messiaen actually uses a polytonal chord derived from Golaud's theme from Debussy's opera in movement 2 (*Traité*: 184). The plot shares many elements with the other stories Messiaen used. Its settings include a forest, a castle, and a dark and airless cave, and its love triangle results in the death of Mélisande. The principal citation occurs in movement 8, where Messiaen describes vertiginous music with reference to a particular experience of Pelléas: "Like Pelléas in the cellars of the old castle, we are seized with vertigo – a vertigo on a higher scale, a vertigo between heaven and earth, a vertigo of death and love, the fear of the unfathomable and of mystery" (*Traité*: 312).

7. Romeo and Juliet

Given that Messiaen's father translated Shakespeare into French, it is perhaps surprising that this version of the supreme love story doesn't feature more. The plot is another love triangle, which culminates in the tragic death of both Romeo and Juliet. Messiaen uses one short quote from the play to describe the emotion and content of movement 5 (see #4 in the literary sources that follow).

8. Folklore of the Cape Verde Islands

In movement 2 Messiaen cites part of a folk tale he attributes to having originated in the Cape Verde Islands, west of Senegal, which parallels the Medusa story. Messiaen's citation is not specific, and the elements he describes occur in several folk tales.[15] They describe how a protagonist will die if they eat certain fruits and the person who has knowledge of this will turn into marble starting from the toes to the knees, then to the waist, then to the shoulders, and finally including the head if they warn the protagonist. Messiaen describes the evil person as a witch and quotes them saying "whoever repeats my words will become marble from head to toe!" (*Traité*: 174).

---

[15] The story can be found in several examples collected in
https://quod.lib.umich.edu/g/genpub/AGY7779.0001.001?rgn=main;view=fulltext.

9. Hindu Asuras

In movement 8 brief mention is made of the giant Asuras of Hindu mythology. These beings are described as demigods and can have either good or bad qualities; however, since Messiaen's reference is made in passing, we have no further details about their meaning. We can speculate that perhaps they possess similar forbidding qualities to the Venus statue and are linked with the more terrifying aspects of love that are embedded in Messiaen's surreal storyline.

B – Literary Sources

1. Rainer Maria Rilke (1875–1926) was an Austrian poet whose ten *Duino Elegies*, written over a period of ten years, are considered his most important work. Messiaen quotes Rilke three times in his analysis of *Turangalîla* (see *Traité*: 153, 282, 322). The most important of these is a quotation from the *Eighth Elegy* in the introduction to his analysis where Messiaen invokes Rilke's concept of "open eternity," which contrasts the real world by being a "Nowhere void of negation, a pure / Unsurveillance that can be inhaled, / forever known and thus not craved."[16] Messiaen quotes a passage at length:

> As children
> we lose ourselves to this in silence, until
> abruptly shaken. Or someone dying *is* it,
> and, near death, does not see death but stares
> beyond it, his gaze perhaps large as the mammals'.
> And lovers, if their partner didn't block
> the view, could then draw near and be astonished . . . (*Traité*: 153).

Messiaen provides his own interpretation of this, describing the union of two lovers in a way that transcends mundane reality and expresses the joy of infinite love:

> They rush towards each other and get lost. It's like a jump into infinity. There is no longer such and such a man and such a woman, but only one exceptional creature, whose halves want to join together, in search of the primitive Androgyne. In this quest, distraught by love, overwhelmed, submerged by a feeling too great in which they are irresponsible actors, unconscious heroes, they reach the dazzling, blinding, total and definitive lightning strike of Joy (Ibid.).

2. Prosper Mérimée (1803–70) was a French historian and writer known for his plays and short stories. "La Vénus d'Ille" was written between 1835 and 1837 and tells of a bronze statue of Venus that comes to life and kills the son of the

---

[16] Translated from the German by Alfred Corn. https://poems.com/poem/the-eighth-elegy/.

statue's owner in the middle of the night. The son is to be married and has absentmindedly left his wedding ring on the finger of the statue. Venus finds him and kills him while he is consummating the marriage. This story is the inspiration for the first cyclic theme of the symphony, which Messiaen refers to as the statue theme.

2. Edgar Allan Poe (1809–49) was an American poet and short-story writer known for his work in horror and mystery. First published in 1843, *The Pit and the Pendulum* tells the narrator's experience of torture during the Spanish Inquisition, facing a swinging blade while propped over a deep pit. Poe's short story *Ligeia* was first published in 1838 and features a narrator who falls in love with a woman named Ligeia. When she dies, he marries a woman named Rowena. She, too, grows ill and dies, but the narrator experiences her revival not as Rowena but as Ligeia, the one with whose memory he had always been obsessed. Specific mention is made in movements 7 and 8 (*Traité*: 297, 312, 331).

3. Paul Éluard (1895–1952) was a French surrealist poet who explored the movement between dream and reality as a challenge to rationalism. Messiaen quotes from several works by Éluard: *Une longue réflexion amoureuse* (1945), *L'amour La Poésie* (1929), "L'Amoureuse," which was included in *Capitale de la douleur* (1926), and "Médieuses," from *Le livre ouvert (1938–1940)*. Notably, he uses a quotation by Éluard to describe the flower theme: "It has two voices, it is double. 'And the light binds the night, the flesh, the earth – The bottomless light of an abandoned body – And of two eyes which are repeated'" (*Traité*: 159).

4. André Breton (1896–1966) was a writer and poet and cofounder of the surrealist movement. Despite Breton's prominence as a surrealist, Messiaen quotes him only once (along with Éluard and Shakespeare) in *Turangalîla* as part of the program for the fifth movement, citing a passage from "L'union libre" published in *Poèmes* (1948). Messiaen describes the movement as a "long and frantic dance of joy," and uses the quotations to help describe the union of two lovers as an epic transformation (*Traité*: 235).

C – Visual Sources

Messiaen's visual inspirations are either paintings or significant monuments and represent a diverse array of sources. Being part of a surrealist description, the connections between them are not immediately obvious, and some are only mentioned in passing, but we are able to make some broad correlations between these disparate elements by the contexts in which Messiaen mentions them.

1. Hieronymus Bosch (1450–1516) was a Dutch painter whose work often explored the human tendency toward temptation and evil, his paintings famously difficult to interpret and sometimes attributed with secret meanings. In movement 6, Messiaen refers to the lovers in a crystal bubble from the renowned painting *The Garden of Earthly Delights* (Figure 2), a triptych completed around 1515 that contains religious themes of creation, temptation, and fall, expressed in a dreamlike state of fantasy and pleasure (*Traité*: 153, 275).

2. Leonardo da Vinci (1452–1519) was an artist and inventor. Messiaen briefly invokes the *Mona Lisa* (1519) (Figure 3), the famous painting by da Vinci that features a profile of a woman with an enigmatic expression (*Traité*: 281). He also describes two other features of Da Vinci's paintings in movement 8 that have musical counterparts: knots of feminine hair and water whirlpools (*Traité*: 326).

3. Marc Chagall (1887–1985) was a French painter whose work often included surrealist elements. By placing subjects upside-down or defying gravity, he represented a whimsical dreamlike inner space (Figure 4). Messiaen was drawn to these images explaining that "where lovers fly away: they have their own myth, and their aerial joy overcame the laws of gravity: here they are gone above the clouds to the search for new planets: the protective fairy blew on them, they flew away like birds" (movement 10, *Traité*: 372). Messiaen also explains that this influenced part of the text in the *Cinq rechants*: "Lovers fly away / Brangien, in space you blow / lovers fly away / to the stars of death … " (*Traité*: 152).

Figure 2 Bosch – The garden of earthly delights (detail)

Figure 3 Da Vinci – Mona Lisa

Figure 4 Chagall – The birthday (1915)

4. Roland Penrose (1900–84) was a British artist associated with the surrealist movement. Messiaen described his painting *Seeing is believing* (or *L'Île invisible*) as "the symbol for the whole of *Harawi*" (Goléa, 1961: 150). In his *Turangalîla* analysis, Messiaen invokes this image during what he describes as the climax of the entire symphony in movement 8 at [R42] (see what follows). The painting is currently in a private collection but can be seen online.[17]

5. Giovanni Battista Piranesi (1720–78) was an architect and artist. In movement 8, Messiaen describes "the dark stairs of Piranesi," probably referring to the

Figure 5 Giovanni Battista Piranesi – The Drawbridge, from *Carceri d'Invenzione*

[17] www.christies.com/en/lot/lot-5164878.

set of sixteen prints of fictitious prisons (*Carceri d'Invenzione*) Piranesi drew, which have elaborate staircases in architectural situations that are not physically possible (Figure 5). Messiaen's reference describes dense and complicated music comprising ostinati over a triple rhythmic canon (*Traité*: 326).

6. The Sphinx of Giza in Egypt depicts the body of a lion and the adorned head of a human that is missing its nose (Figure 6). It dates to the 3rd millennium BCE. As with the following five examples, Messiaen makes very few direct references to these buildings and statues, but often includes them in groups and finds them fascinating for their inherent monumentality. The reference to the Sphinx comes at the end of the description of movement 5: "The Sphinx of Giza (Egypt), the stepped pyramid of the Temple of the Warriors at Chichen Itza (Mexico) better still: some immense and solitary mountain or some terrible abyss, that is what is evoked here – granitic or abyssal – the enormous and heavy thirds of the statue theme!" (*Traité*: 273).

7. The stepped pyramid of the Temple of the Warriors is located in Chichen Itza, a Mayan city founded in the sixth century CE in the Yucatan Peninsula of Mexico (Figure 7). Messiaen refers to the endless stairs of *El Castillo*, which has 91 stairs on each side for a total of 365 when the top platform is included. In addition to the citation just noted, the Temple of the Warriors is mentioned at the end of movement 1 where Messiaen describes the combination of timbres as having "the roughness simple and terrifying of certain monuments of Maya

Figure 6 The Sphinx

Figure 7 The Temple of the Warriors

art, such as the 'Pyramid of Inscriptions' of Palenque, [and] the 'Temple of the Warriors' of Chichen Itza, with the decorative brutality of their endless stairs" (*Traité*: 169).

8. The Temple of Inscriptions of Palenque in Chiapas, Mexico is a stepped pyramid that was a funerary monument (Figure 8). It is notable for the hiero-glyphic texts in Maya script found both inside and outside the temple and is mentioned only once by Messiaen in the quotation just cited.

9. The Winged Lions in Nanjing, China, are sculptures of mythical hybrid animals found at the tomb of Xiao-Xiu (475–518) (Figure 9). Known as auspi-cious creatures with magical powers, they were part of a collection at this site that included four steles supported by stone tortoises, and a pair of fluted columns. Messiaen refers to them, along with the Tenayuca serpents, Easter Island heads, and a quote from a Senegalese myth, in his description of music in movement 2:

> We think of such heavy and terrifying figures: the 'Winged lion of Xiao-Xiu' (near Nanjing, China), the 'sun serpent' of Tenayuca (Mexico), the huge stone heads of Easter Island (Polynesia). We think of this tale from the Cape Verde Islands (west of Senegal) where the witch after each harmful gift adds: "Whoever repeats my words will become marble from head to toe!" (*Traité*: 174).

10. The serpents of Tenayuca are a pair of stone carvings of coiled serpents outside the pyramid of Tenayuca near Mexico City (Figure 10). The pyramid was constructed in phases from the early 1200s to the early 1500s by the Chichimec people.

Figure 8 The Temple of Inscriptions

Figure 9 The Winged Lions of Xiao-Xiu

Figure 10 The Serpents of Tenayuca

Figure 11 The stone heads (Moai) of Easter Island

11. The stone heads of Easter Island (a dependency of Chile) are thought to date from the eighth to to the eleventh centuries CE and represent persons who were posthumously deified (Figure 11). They share some characteristics with pre-Incan monuments on the South American continent.

Other specific programmatic elements mentioned by Messiaen include mountains, deserts, waterfalls, the abyss, Mayan art (in general), caves, dinosaurs, Chinese poetry, and flowers (orchid, fuchsia, gladiolus, and convolvulus). He also refers to the embedded meaning of Hindu rhythms, citing, for example, the meanings of laksmîça and râgavardhana in movement 1.

Taken as a whole, this is a disparate selection of images; however, they point to both the beautiful and terrible aspects of the love Messiaen describes. His preoccupation is the notion that two lovers become a single entity through an overwhelming and superhuman love (as evoked by the potion drunk by Tristan and Isolde). He also describes the darker side of love, noting that it often involves death and has terrifying aspects that Messiaen connects with several dark stories and images.

Sometimes connecting a composer's life and their works can be a useful analytical tool, and many scholars have pointed to connections with Messiaen's personal circumstances and the love themes in the trilogy (see, for example, Simeone, 2002: 106). The mental and physical decline of his first wife Claire Delbos must have had an enormous impact on Messiaen; however, since he does not explicitly connect his personal life and his music, I have not included discussion of that element in this analysis.

5 Analysis and Explanation of the *Turangalîla-symphonie*

Although Bruhn (2008: 199) and Sherlaw Johnson (1975: 24) have suggested ways of grouping the movements that might point to connections that help the listener, the following sections present the movements of the symphony in order since there is a sense of journey through the piece, and presenting the information in sequence will help the reader connect with the listening experience. Musicologists and theorists have provided analyses of movements that differ from Messiaen's. The analysis presented here takes as its starting point Messiaen's own writings, since this helps us to understand his compositional process and provides insight into specific aspects of the score that only the composer is able to explain. Prior to the analysis of each movement, it is necessary to understand four principal themes used throughout the symphony, which Messiaen described as "cyclical," and which are initially described as archetypes.

Four Cyclical Themes

Turangalîla uses four main themes, identified and described by Messiaen himself, which are subjected to a high degree of manipulation. Three have symbolic significance and names: statue theme, flower theme, and love theme.

The fourth Messiaen simply describes as the chord theme, which carries no symbolic function but is foundational for much of the music and is more easily identifiable in its different forms because Messiaen has labeled the archetype. Messiaen himself describes these themes as "cyclic" because they occur throughout the work; however, there are many other themes in the symphony, some of which are more or less related to the four named themes. Named themes should be easily aurally identifiable, so Messiaen has distinguished the cyclic themes by various musical means (including instrumentation, speed, dynamic, and so on), and provided visual and literary allusions that help to explain their roles in the program.

The four cyclic themes are produced here in their archetypal form along with Messiaen's description of each taken from the liner notes to the 1991 Deutsche Grammaphon recording.

1. The statue theme

> *The first cyclic theme, in weighty thirds, nearly always played by trombones fortissimo, has that oppressive, terrifying brutality of Mexican ancient monuments. For me it has always evoked some dread and fatal statue (one thinks of Prosper Mérimée's 'La Vénus d'Ille').*

Example 2 The statue theme archetype
www.cambridge.org/Shenton

As noted previously, in the *Traité* Messiaen elaborates on the Mexican monuments he refers to here. Coupled with the Mérimée story, this theme denotes for Messiaen a terrifying nightmare depicting another side to the love he is trying to portray between two humans. The theme is characterized by its heavy thirds played in octaves and accented.

2. The flower theme

> *The second cyclic theme, assigned to caressing clarinets in a pianissimo, is in two parts, like two eyes reflecting each other ... Here the most appropriate image is that of a flower. One might think of a delicate orchid, a florid fuchsia, a red gladiolus, an excessively pliant convolvulus.*

Example 3 The flower theme archetype
www.cambridge.org/Shenton

Figure 12 Gladiolus

In contrast to the heavy statue theme, the delicate flower theme is a quiet motif in two parts, consisting of three grace notes in each voice moving to a chord that increases from a minor second to a major second, then a minor third in each measure. Messiaen envisages a series of symmetrical flowers including the gladiolus whose flowers are set out on the stem in a way that is described in the music (Figure 12).

3. The love theme

The third cyclic theme is the most important of all. It is the love theme.

Example 4 The love theme archetype
www.cambridge.org/Shenton

Starting on a C-sharp seventh chord, this theme is full of rich added chords and is usually presented at a slow speed. It is stated most prominently as a chorale throughout movement 6.

4. The chord theme

The fourth cyclic theme is a simple chain of chords. More than a theme, it is a pretext for different sound strata: it makes possible, for example, the opposition between rhythmic chords in changing registers on the solo piano and these same chords, scattered by crossing counterpoints into every colour of the orchestra, at the beginning and end of the eighth movement. There and elsewhere, whether it is hurled into the depths in heavy bundles of blackness, or distributed in fine strokes, in airy arpeggios, this "chords theme" embodies the formula of the alchemists' doctrine: "dissociate and coagulate."

Example 5 The chord theme archetype
www.cambridge.org/Shenton

These four chords are the basis of much of the musical material in the symphony. The ways Messiaen composes using these chords involves a new technique. In his reference to the alchemists, Messiaen uses the Latin phrase "Solve et coagula," a quote from medieval alchemy that means to break a substance down into its basic elements before forming it into something new. The chord theme archetype contains the basic elements from which new musical compounds are created.

Analysis by Movement

Most of Messiaen's techniques can be worked out through close analysis of the score, and many of these are noted in the 1990 version of the score. For others, such as programmatic ideas, we rely on Messiaen's own descriptions in the *Traité* and elsewhere. In the following analyses, each movement is prefaced by Messiaen's own short program note for the premiere of the work, which serves to point out how little of the

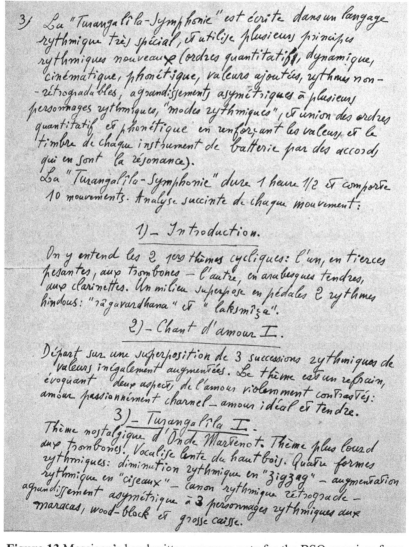

Figure 13 Messiaen's handwritten program note for the BSO premiere from their archive

technical or programmatic elements of the music were actually available to that audience (and this, in part, might account for many of the negative feelings expressed about the premiere) (see Figures 13 and 14). The aim of this analysis of the *Turangalîla-symphonie* is to highlight innovative and essential musical and programmatic elements so that the reader will get a broad understanding of the work and of Messiaen's specific techniques. The music is generally described by using rehearsal numbers (designated [R1] and so on), which delineate major sections, but occasional detail is provided by page number and measure since the measures are not numbered in the score. Since the 1990 version uses the same pagination as the 1953 score, either can be used, though the later one is preferable since it identifies many of the compositional devices. Information attributed to Messiaen is from the *Turangalîla* section of *Traité* 2 unless otherwise noted.[18]

Movement 1 – *Introduction* [Introduction] (*modéré, un peu vif* [moderately, somewhat lively])[19]

The first two cyclic themes are heard: One in ponderous thirds from the trombones – the other in gentle arabesques from the clarinets. Two Hindu rhythms are superimposed in pedals: rāgavardhana, and laksmîça.

According to Messiaen, the Introduction has the form A, B, C, A, where A is a presentation of the first two cyclical themes; B is a piano cadenza linking A to C; C is a long polyrhythm using the gamelan group; and the final A is an abbreviated repeat of the opening, which serves as a conclusion.

Messiaen chose a bold opening to the symphony, with driving sixteenth notes in the strings responded to by chords in various groupings of the wind and brass. At [R2] the statue theme played fortissimo by the trombones is heard against string and piano trills. At [R4] a fan arabesque in the piano, wind, ondes, and strings emulates a feeling of vertigo like a "waterfall with eddies at the bottom of the abyss," using music derived from two movements of *Harawi* ("Syllables," a short love song to Isolde, and "Katchikatchi," a paean to the stars).

Two measures before [R8], a sequence of four chords is played tutti (see Example 6).

---

[18] Note on the translation from French: in the *Traité* Messiaen often uses note form with incomplete and fragmentary passages linked by ellipses or dashes. For clarity these have been translated into complete sentences and, where a word or phrase is difficult to translate, the original French has been placed in parentheses.

[19] It is tricky to translate the nuance of some French tempo markings, so I have opted for a rather literal translation in some cases.

Example 6 Sequence of chords around [R8]
www.cambridge.org/Shenton

Messiaen described these chords as follows: Group A is a "verticalization and concentration" of chords from his large piano cycle *Vingt Regards* (1944), and subsequently reused in *Cinq rechants* for the text "lîla, lîla, ma mémoire – ma caresse." For Group B, the first chord is a quintuple appoggiatura on the second, and the second chord is a dominant ninth on an E-flat bass note. For group C they are a chord on an appoggiaturized dominant on a common bass note (C♯); and for Group D they are a transposition of Group B. Here Messiaen again refers to the movement "Amour oiseau d'étoile" from *Harawi*, which occurs frequently in his description of *Turangalîla* (though it is not clear if any programmatic elements are also implied for the Introduction).

At [R8] a short theme for oboes and cor anglais with solo cello prepares for the flower theme, pianissimo on clarinets, at [R9]. From [R10] to [R12], the chord sequence in Example 6 is developed in different ways including transposition, truncation, and retrograde. The linking piano cadenza at [R11] opens with an upward movement, is comprised of short phrases based on the two stated themes and the chord groups, and closes with a downward movement.

After the exposition of the first two named themes of the symphony (statue and flower), the main part of the movement occurs between [R12] and [R20] and comprises a "combination and superposition of various musics, rhythms and various modes: polyrhythm, polymodality, polymusic" (*Traité*: 163). Messiaen hints at the complexity of the music, derived through combination and superposition, by using the term "poly." The principal music is an ostinato in the gamelan group (supported by a few other instruments) that includes silences of various lengths and which is identified in the texture by its "crystalline" attacks. Two further ostinati are superimposed over this texture. The first uses the Hindu rhythm lakskmîça. Messiaen notes that it means "calm as the peace which descends from the goddess Lakshmî," and that the rhythm is based on the principle of inexact augmentation. The second uses the rhythm râgavardhana, which is translated as "rhythm which gives the most life to the râga." Râgavardhana contains several elements that Messiaen develops: reduction and end-to-end increase, and the alchemists' technique of "coagulation or dissociation," which allows him to reconstruct new music from the basic elements of the original (such as the addition of a dot, inaccurate decrease, and nonretrogradable elements). The result is a rhythm that is complexly notated in 2/4 time in the score, but which sounds to the listener like a simple ostinato (see Example 7). The juxtaposition of these two contrasting Hindu rhythms parallels the juxtaposition of the love theme and statue theme indicating perhaps how closely love and terror cohabit.

Example 7 Râgavardhana (original form) and the rhythm Messiaen derived
from it

The shortened reprise of the opening section begins at [R21] with the statue theme, combined with the descending music using a chromatic duration heard at [R7], and is followed by the chord sequence heard two measures before [R8] (Example 6).

The opening movement does not serve as a traditional exposition of all the elements of the symphony. The main programmatic elements of this movement are not love but terror. The statue theme is at the forefront, and the final section is described by Messiaen using language that invokes dread and horror: "These combinations have the simple and terrifying roughness of some monuments of Mayan art, such as the Pyramid of Inscriptions of Palenque, or the Temple of the Warriors of Chichen Itza, with the decorative brutality of their endless stairs" (*Traité*: 169).

Movement 2 – *Chant d'amour I* [Love song 1] (*modéré, lourd* [moderately, heavy])

This movement begins with the superimposing of three rhythmic successions of values in unequal augmentation. The theme is a refrain, evoking two aspects of love in violent contrast: impassioned earthly love – ideal and tender love.

The first of the three love movements carries over some of the violent themes from the Introduction using similar visual imagery and musical devices, but contrasts it with a more lyrical evocation representing a depiction of ideal love. Messiaen described the form as a refrain with two verses and development, and provided the following summary (*Traité*: 171):

1. Short introduction superimposing three rhythmic sequences, of which the respective durations are unevenly increased.

2. to [R4]: refrain in F-sharp major, alternating two elements: (a) passionate motif by the trumpets, (b) tender motif by the ondes and strings.

3. to [R9]: first verse.

4. to [R13]: refrain in F-sharp major.

5. to [R18]: second verse, interjected several times by a three-chord motif that is violently carnal.

6. to [R28]: refrain, reduced to just the antecedent part of the previous passionate motif on the trumpets.

7. to [R29]: development, by melodic repetitions with different transpositions of detail between them, symmetrically taking up these differences at each term. These processes are applied simultaneously at the start of the refrain in perpetual sixteenth notes in the strings, and a descending movement in eighth-notes in the brass.

8. big expansion [montée] on the ternary carnal motif, to [R34]. This expansion constitutes the second element of the development.

9. to [R36]: third element of the development, which is an implied dominant pedal on C-sharp. It uses all the chords of the introduction, alternating between woodwind/brass and piano. Superimposed on these chords, the strings and the ondes repeat a melodic fragment of the refrain, with different transpositions of detail, taking up these differences symmetrically at each term.

10. to [R40]: Coda.

The short introduction is comprised of three successions of superimposed chords played fortissimo and distributed among different groups in the orchestra. Messiaen notes that the "rhythm, instrumentation and dissonance are perfectly cruel," and he provides some very specific visual imagery to further describe the music:

> We think of such heavy and terrifying figures as the winged lion of Xiao-Xiu (near Nanjing, China); the sun serpents from Tenayuca (Mexico); and the immense stone heads of Easter Island (Polynesia). We think of this tale of the Cape Verde Islands (west of Senegal) where the witch after each harmful donation adds: "whoever repeats my words will become marble from head to toe!" (*Traité*: 174).

In the refrain starting at [R4], Messiaen describes the sequence of chords as "the bells of loving nostalgia," found in two movements ("Adieu" and "Syllables") in *Harawi*. Seven measures after [R4] there is a graceful piano melody, which he likens to the "disjoint intervals" of Chopin and which he reuses in the third development section. The other music here is based on the chord theme and combined with a phrase played by the violins and violas (colored by the ondes using the ribbon setting).

For Messiaen, the alternation of two types of love summarizes both the movement and the entire symphony:

> All the work is made of the alternation or fusion of two loves: one, violent, passionate, carnal; the other, ideal, dreamy, airy. Like a hermaphrodite, it combines mineral power with vegetal flexibility. Magically, it opposes the bewitchments of reality and of dreams. And always, with the union of lovers, poetry, the fairytale that surround it, even to the treasures of the archetypes of Love. "Our eyes return to their source / Under the bare flesh of their native beauty" (Paul Éluard: *Une longue réflexion amoureuse*) (*Traité*: 176).

Messiaen frequently borrows from himself without noting whether any connection should be made between the different versions of the music. This is important where there is either a text or a defined program associated with the original piece that may have prompted Messiaen's use in a subsequent work. In this movement Messiaen makes explicit some connections with *Cinq rechants* when he describes some of the arabesques that ornament music played two octaves apart "like Mozart" by the oboe and bassoon:

> The second melodic ornamentation … and the beginning of the fourth are found in the feminine curves of the *Cinq rechants*, emphasizing these words: "octopus with golden tentacles," in the fifth *Rechant*; and in the third: "tender robe," and "all the beauty of the new landscape" (*Traité*: 179).

Messiaen also reuses material that has no programmatic connotations such as the new melody heard at [R26] on the piccolo, flute, and oboe which can also be found in the next movement of *Turangalîla* and in the *Cinq rechants*.

The second refrain of this movement ([R13] to [R17]) is a repeat of the music starting at [R4] and leads into the second chorus, which has new music with the character of a lullaby that puts the lovers to sleep. In this music Messiaen identifies a melodic counterpoint played on the gamelan instruments (glockenspiel and celesta), which is repeated every 19 notes and is played alongside a rhythmic counterpoint on the wood block. The wood block music is itself comprised of the Hindu rhythms gajajhampa and vijaya, and the fourth Greek epitrite (a metrical foot comprised of three long syllables followed by one short syllable).

Occasionally, Messiaen notes a passage that has an extramusical character that is not directly related to a programmatic element but supports the general sound world of the movement or section. At one measure before [R19], for example, he notes "under the brassy sound of the horns, the low woodwind, in rapid detached chords in parallel seconds and sevenths, make a very particular cackling" (*Traité*: 182).

In most movements Messiaen includes a development section. In this movement it begins at [R29] and uses three specific elements: a double development on the opening material of the refrain, a cataclysmic ascent and descent of the violently carnal motif heard in the second verse, and an ostinato of bells over fragments of the refrain that are treated in repetitions and symmetrical variants.

Much of the music in this movement is mathematically derived, but there are occasional hints about the origination of some of the ideas. For example, three measures before [R32] the horns play a polytonal chord derived from Golaud's theme in Debussy's opera *Pelléas et Mélisande*, and at [R32] he describes an opening fan procedure using two superimposed melodies. Of these, the first is derived from a Russian folk cadence that is transformed by diminution and augmentation.

Movement 3 – *Turangalîla I* [Turangalîla 1] (*presque lent, rêveur* [almost slow, dreamily])

A nostalgic theme from the ondes Martenot. A heavier theme from the trombones. A slow melody from the oboe. Four rhythmic patterns: rhythmic diminution in "zigzag," rhythmic augmentation in "scissors" [crossed], reversed rhythmic canon, asymmetric augmentation of three rhythmic characters by the maracas, wood block, and bass drum.

The first *Turangalîla* movement opens slowly and quietly with a conversational duet between a clarinet and the ondes, supported by chimes from the bells and vibraphone (opening to [R2]). This is the first theme. The second theme is presented in the bass and low brass at a faster tempo, against two other musical ideas: glissandi on the cello and ondes, and an agitated counterpoint superimposed using the gamelan ensemble. It appears in two stanzas: the first between [R2] and [R4], the second (an inverted variation) between [R9] and [R12]. This theme uses a Greek iambic rhythm, which is presented five different ways, starting with the basic iambic pattern of short, long (*Traité*: 193):

a) short, long: ♪ ♩

b) adding a dot to the short and long durations: ♪. ♩.

c) adding a dot to the short, removing 1/4 of the length of the long, which gives two equal values: ♪. ♩.

d) the short note is normal length [i.e. one sixteenth], the long is very elongated (to the value of seven sixteenth notes); the latter is followed by another note with a value of six sixteenths: ♪ ♩. ♪♩.

e) addition of a dot to the short and the long, but the long is formed as two short values, so there are, in total, three values of three sixteenth notes: ♩. ♩. ♩.

In the first stanza the five rhythmic variants are presented in this order: a – b – a – a – c – c – d – c – c – d – a – e – a – a. Although there are palindromic sets within this sequence, it is unlikely that any mathematical procedure is foundational in the creation of the order.

For this section Messiaen provides a glimpse of the visual imagery of this music, associating it with the landscape and soundscape of Tibet:

> The whole of section 2, in stark contrast to the nostalgia, the desert loneliness of the first page, seems to mix the Balinese gamelan and the immense horns [dungchens] of the Tibetan lamas, for some initiatory and terrifying ceremony; in the background of the scene, the snow and the sun of the Himalayas, and an old memory of the wind and the sea (*Traité*: 194).

From [R4] to [R5] Messiaen uses his technique of "chromatic durations" in which a rhythm is presented in augmentation in the horns and woodwind on a four-chord ostinato while simultaneously a rhythm is presented in diminution in the second violins and cellos on another four-chord ostinato. Example 8 gives the rhythm as it appears in its augmented version. The value of each rhythm is given as a number of sixteenth notes. Instead of increasing each by one sixteenth cumulatively, Messiaen complicates the process by moving alternately from a sequence that moves from one sixteenth to eight sixteenths with a second sequence that moves from five sixteenths to 12 sixteenths. This means that the values 5, 6, 7, and 8 are duplicated in the complete pattern.

Example 8 Rhythmic augmentation in *Turangalîla I*, 2–4

The strings play the same rhythm but in reverse, starting at the 11-value pitch. This is a clear example of Messiaen's "fan" [éventail] procedure since it resembles the opening and closing of a fan.

The other principal compositional techniques described by Messiaen in this movement include the following:

- A pizzicato motif for solo double bass which starts on C-sharp[4] at [R1] and recurs at [R5], [R7], and at the end [R13].

- A fan-like retrograde rhythmic canon in the oboe and flute/clarinet from [R6] to [R8], which is the third theme.
- A fourth theme from [R6] to [R9], comprised of three rhythmic characters taken by three instruments, which are as follows: the bass drum increases, the maracas decrease, the wood block stays the same. Messiaen distinguishes the sound of each:

Maracas – mineral timbre, sneezed, rustling and crackling, small pebbles, small pellets, maracas.
Wood block – vegetable timbre, clear, clean, frank, resonant, reminiscent of the beak of the Great Spotted Woodpecker on tree bark.
Bass drum – animal timbre, dull, deaf, deep, subterranean pulsation of the bass drum.

Messiaen also provides his color associations for each of these: "the bass drum is black as night – the wood block is light green, a fresh and youthful tint, a kind of chartreuse green – the maracas pull on yellow and red ochres." For Messiaen the color associations with timbre are important "because it makes it possible to identify with certainty each rhythmic character" (*Traité*: 200). For the listener, the sound differentiation does make it possible to distinguish the different elements, though the audience may not make the same color associations as Messiaen.

At the end of his detailed analysis, Messiaen provides a further example of the imagery the music conjures for him (or perhaps the imagery he wished to conjure for the listener), noting: "The cold, the night, descend on the orchestra, in a supermundane inter-planetary mystery, extended into silence by a dying sound from the ondes" (*Traité*: 207).

Movement 4 – *Chant d'amour II* [Love song 2] (*bien modéré* [well moderated])

A scherzo with two trios. The trios are very songful [chantants]; the melodic line is voluptuously undulating and tender. In the da capo, the scherzo and the two trios are superimposed, thus erecting a threefold music.

Messiaen's very close attention to timbres and his intuitive ideas to manipulate sounds is quite remarkable. In the opening of the second love song movement, for example, he noted that the sound of the piccolo and bassoon was "a little dry, a little skeletal," and felt it needed more ambiance. To enhance the sound, he added "the metallic resonance of the suspended cymbal, and the small clusters of seconds minor (sustained and vibrated sounds) of the vibraphone," and couched the results in poetic terms:

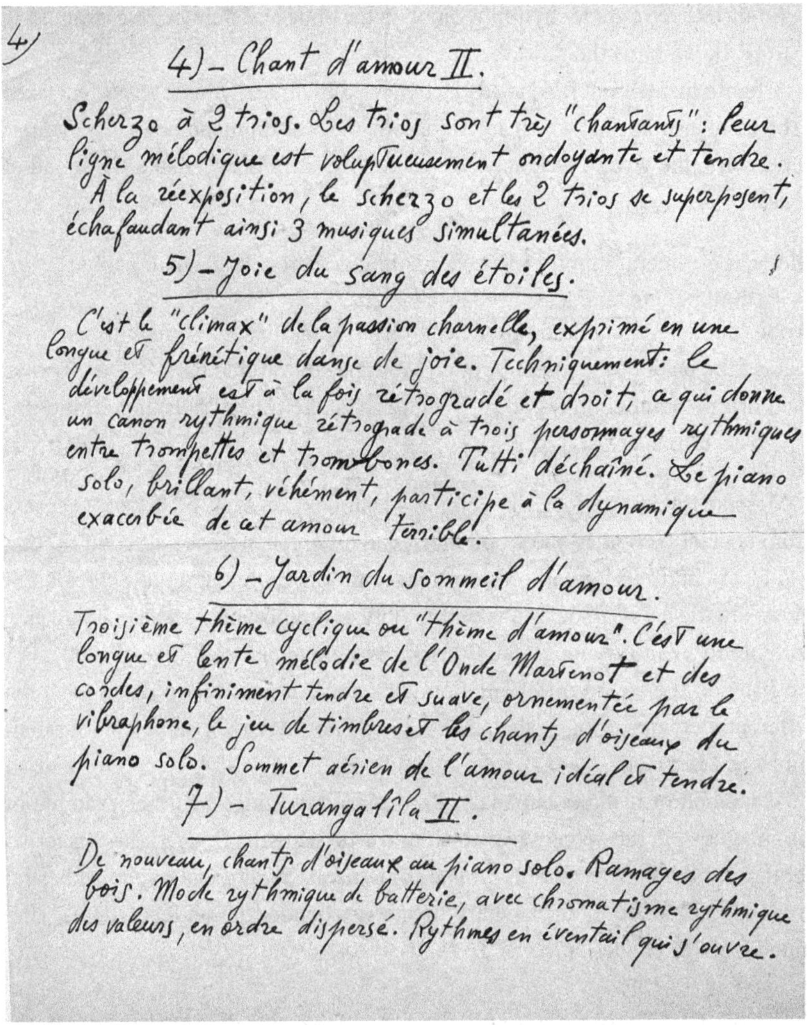

4) – Chant d'amour II.

Scherzo à 2 trios. Les trios sont très "chantants": leur ligne mélodique est voluptueusement ondoyante et tendre. À la réexposition, le scherzo et les 2 trios se superposent, échafaudant ainsi 3 musiques simultanées.

5) – Joie du sang des étoiles.

C'est le "climax" de la passion charnelle, exprimé en une longue et frénétique danse de joie. Techniquement: le développement est à la fois rétrogradé et droit, ce qui donne un canon rythmique rétrograde à trois personnages rythmiques entre trompettes et trombones. Tutti déchaîné. Le piano solo, brillant, véhément, participe à la dynamique exacerbée de cet amour terrible.

6) – Jardin du sommeil d'amour.

Troisième thème cyclique ou "thème d'amour". C'est une longue et lente mélodie de l'Onde Martenot et des cordes, infiniment tendre et suave, ornementée par le vibraphone, le jeu de timbres et les chants d'oiseaux du piano solo. Sommet aérien de l'amour idéal et tendre.

7) – Turangalîla II.

De nouveau, chants d'oiseaux au piano solo. Ramages des bois. Mode rythmique de batterie, avec chromatisme rythmique des valeurs, en ordre dispersé. Rythmes en éventail qui s'ouvre.

Figure 14 Messiaen's BSO program note for movements 4 to 7

Between the high treble of the piccolo and the bass of the bassoon, the suspended cymbal sets up its midrange attacks, and the vibraphone spreads the vibrato of its siren voices, the high medium of its crystal harmonies, the prolonged poetry of its resonances, evoking the shock of stalactites and calcite draperies, the air currents of the oracle caves (*Traité*: 211).[20]

---

[20] These "grottes oracliennes" (presumably the caves of the Oracle of Delphi) are also mentioned in the program for movement XI of *Vingt regards*.

Messiaen summarized this movement as being in nine sections:

1. Scherzo for piccolo and bassoon, with a rhythmic theme on the wood block.
2. Bridge.
3. Refrain and first trio on the woodwind.
4. Second trio on solo strings.
5. Superposition of the two trios, of woodwind and strings, with birdsongs on the piano.
6. Bridge.
7. Reprise and superposition of the scherzo, the two trios and the statue theme. All elements of the movement are heard at the same time, in a complex scaffolding of ten simultaneous musics.
8. Solo piano cadenza.
9. Coda. The flower theme is heard on the clarinets, pianissimo, the statue theme on the trombones, fortissimo, the refrain on the ondes and solo violins. The end is worth noting, with the effect of a fan closing and opening in the vibraphone and the piano, over the calm and unctuous surface of three trombones playing pianissimo (*Traité*: 209).

A rhythmic ostinato on the wood block starts in measure 5 (returning at [R14]), which is comprised of three Hindu rhythms that Messiaen also uses elsewhere in the symphony: râgavardhana, candrakalâ (in diminution), and lakskmîça (in augmentation). Although the ostinato is only played *mf* and is embedded in increasingly dense music, Messiaen asserts that it is a theme, even though it is only a rhythm and single pitch.

The fifth section (the superimposition of the two trios) Messiaen described as "two complete musical ideas walking together, each having its own rhythm, melody, harmony, timbre." To this he added a third musical element. The piano from the seventh measure of [R8] to [R11] has a birdsong passage comprised of eight stanzas that "present in rapid and numerous arabesques all kinds of melodic designs and contours, often turned towards the treble, and always inverting more or less the same notes, in a great pattern of intervals, like a more fanciful raga, primitive, with a little triumph, a little mockery, a lot of life, cheerfulness, imagination, and an incessantly renewed invention." Messiaen also noted how he felt this influenced the other music around it: "Melodic color, modal color, rhythmic color, interval and attack color, all characteristics of the Blackbird, allowing the piano solo to impose its brilliance, its diamond coating, its flashes, mix with the themes and timbres of the orchestra, complicate and transform their purple-yellow and blue-orange meanderings by the lights of their little extra sun" (*Traité*: 222).

A second bridge (using the same music as the first but transposed and with the direction of some parts reversed) leads to a complex passage in which Messiaen describes nine superimposed musical elements to which he adds the statue theme for a total of ten separate musical identities:

1. The theme of Scherzo.
2. The features of the Piano solo.
3. The pizzi of double basses.
4. The gamelan.
5. The rhythmic pedal of the wood block.
6. The rhythm of the small Turkish cymbal.
7. The rhythm of the snare drum.
8. The first trio by woodwind and horns.
9. The second trio with strings.
10. The first cyclical theme with trombones.

Despite their differences, these identities "combine, stir, display, mix, oppose, scaffold, superimpose their colors. Blue-orange, purples, lilacs, reds, turn and interpenetrate in shimmering sinuosities: iridescent maelstrom, torrents of rainbows, slings [écharpes] and suns, all the loves and all the joys" (*Traité*: 227).

The loud cacophony of all these elements dissipates suddenly and is replaced by a cadenza for the solo piano starting at [R16]. Using several harmonic sequences from *Harawi*, the short but virtuosic passage ends with a passage that provides full resonance of the keyboard from bottom to top followed by a sequence of chords that end with a cluster in the upper register of the piano. The coda transitions with a quiet statement of the flower theme, followed by the statue theme accompanied by trilled chords that were heard in the first movement. An echo of the piano cadenza leads to some strange music at [R18] that suggests to Messiaen a place "outside the concert hall," that "gives the illusion of something with poetic distance, like sounds descended from another planet." Here chords from the piano "fall like precious and bluish stones in the water," and lead to the final four measures. These, Messiaen notes, are unremarkable, being formed from simple musical means; however, the effect is like "Shocking stalactites and calcite draperies ... sounds melt mysteriously, like blue moons eaten by the foam of the water, like the memory of the draft in the Oraclian caves ... Down below, calm as the earth, forgotten as the water, soft as the night, the trombones and the horns have not moved" (*Traité*: 233).

Movement 5 – *Joie du sang des étoiles* [*Joy of the Blood of the Stars*]
(*Vif, passionné avec joie* [*fast, passionate, with joy*])

This is the "peak" of carnal passion expressed in a long and frenetic dance of joy. Technically, the development is at once straightforward and reversed, which produces a rhythmical and reversed canon of three rhythmic identities between the trumpets and trombones. The full orchestra is released. The piano solo, brilliant and vehement, participates in the dynamic exacerbation of this terrible love.

Messiaen described the title of this movement as "surreal-looking" and suggested that it "sublimates carnal passion," adding that "this cosmic character of carnal union is expressed here by a hymn to life, to movement, to joy. It's a long and frantic dance of joy!" In a very rare response to criticism, he acknowledged that the movement has been misunderstood: "Prudes found it sensual, dodecaphonists found it tonal: these two adjectives being considered by them as insults!" Despite the criticism, he noted that it found favor with the public, and asserted that "I never wrote anything more alive, more dynamic, more violently in love." He added an equally uncharacteristic boast, suggesting that in this movement "there is here an exploration [*une recherche*] and a complexity in the rhythmic work which should interest technicians a great deal" (*Traité*: 235).

After suggesting that, in general, a musical theme is much less interesting than its development, he notes that in the early performances of the symphony (before musicologists and theorists studied the score) few people noticed whether a particular theme is a transformation of, for example, the statue theme. Nor, he notes, had anyone heard the kind of rhythmic complexity composed in the development section of this movement, which uses the statue theme first with three rhythmic characters, and then with six character rhythms in retrograde canon (*Traité*: 235). As a result of these observations, he added several indications in the 1990 revision of the score regarding some of his compositional processes. In this movement, for example, he notes that the music at the start is a variation of the first cyclic theme (Score: 163). Some of the additional footnotes are very specific about the musical content. At the start of the "grand development" section, Messiaen explains that between [R14] and [R21] the horns and trombones develop the first cyclic theme treated as rhythmic characters. He indicates the three rhythmic characters in the score using the letters A, B, and C, and places a number above each pitch, which indicates the length of each in sixteenth notes. For these three rhythmic characters A increases, B decreases, and C remains the same (Score: 188).

In the *Traité*, this "joy" movement is also prefaced by detailed notes concerning the program. Messiaen begins by asserting, "All true lovers know that the flesh is terrible, beautiful, and separate, when it is the flesh of Tristan, or the flesh of Isolde alone." Quotes from four poets establish the different types of love at work in the movement:

1. Paul Éluard: "There had to be a face / Respond to all the names in the world" (*L'amour la poésie*); and "She has the shape of my hands, / She has the color of my eyes, / She is swallowed up in my shadow / Like a stone on the sky" (*Capitale de la douleur*). The union of true lovers is a transformation, a transformation on a global scale.
2. André Breton finds all the elements in the loved one: "My wife / with eyes at the level of water at the level of air, earth and fire" [*L'union libre*].
3. Shakespeare's lover [Juliet] said: "My bounty is as boundless as the sea" (*Romeo and Juliet*).[21]
4. And Tristan tells Isolde "If all the world were visible to us at once, I would see nothing but you" *(Roman en prose de Tristan)* (*Traité*: 235).

As with the first movement, this movement consists of three parts: an exposition (start to [R13]), a grand development that occupies most of the movement ([R14] to [R37]), and a re-exposition ([R38] to the end).

This movement is interesting because Messiaen expanded the notion of rhythmic characters to include both melodic and harmonic characters and all three are used in this movement. As their names suggest, these new characters are either melodic or harmonic in nature but still adhere to the principle that, if one character acts, then another character must respond as though being acted upon (and, since they are often used in groups of three, a third character remains indifferent to the action). Details of the new characters are noted where they occur in the following list.

A – Exposition

Section 1) Refrain in D-flat major (combined with mode of limited transposition 2), derived from the statue theme using antecedent and consequent phrases.

Section 2) [R4] First couplet using a melody subsequently used in *Cinq rechants* (movement 5). Some of the musical material is derived from three movements of *Harawi* ("La ville qui dormait, toi," "Adieu," and "Syllabes").

Section 3) [R6] Refrain in D-flat major heard once with minor variations in the form of a counterpoint in perpetual sixteenth notes in the gamelan (piano, celesta, and glockenspiel).

---

[21] The quote is from the famous balcony scene and continues: "My love as deep; the more I give to thee, / The more I have, for both are infinite" (Act 2, Scene 2, line 984).

Section 4) [R8] Second couplet using a chord sequence that is repeated in movement 10 of the symphony and a chord sequence later used in *Cinq rechants* on the text "lîla, lîla, my memory, my caress" (movement 3).

Section 5) [R10] Refrain in D-flat major, varied from the first hearing and with a concluding section at [R13], which has a "great concluding feature" in the piano and strings while the horns and percussion modify the rhythm of the D-flat major chord using diminution.

B – Grand development

Section 6) [R14] From [R14] to [R21] the statue theme is developed in the following ways:

a) With the brass (horns and trombones), which treat it as rhythmic characters: A increases, B decreases, and C remains the same.
b) In the woodwind and strings, which develop it as melodic rather than rhythmic characters.
c) In the piano solo, which accompanies the melodic characters of the wood-wind/strings.
d) The combination of these three elements (brass, woodwind and strings, piano solo) creates a harmonic character.

The music is so complicated that in his analysis Messiaen notes that he wrote it in 3/16 time so that the conductor had something regular to beat. The music was, however, conceived without bar lines, so in the *Traité* Messiaen transcribes the music into a simpler form to make it more comprehensible and describes its colors and character:

> The whole of Section 6 is a swirl of colors, where lead gray and mud struggle against shimmers of yellow-purple-red dominated by orange . . . despite all this superimposed music, despite the changes of the harmonic character and all the melodic and rhythmic characters, the whole remains clear, joyful, passionate, and swirls in an ever-increasing dynamism. The rhythmic characters in the brass remain the essential element, we hear them above all: their durations are perpetually underlined by the metallic percus-sions which double them very exactly, the suspended cymbal always sup-porting character B, the Chinese cymbal always supporting the characters A and C (*Traité*: 248).

Section 7) [R21] Refrain in E major, periods 1 and 2 only. As in the exposition, it is played alternately by brass/woodwind and ondes/strings. At the same time, the triangle and suspended cymbal play three Hindu rhythms, râgavardhana (adapted), candrakalâ, and lakskmîça, which were heard in the previous movement.

Section 8) [R23] A transitional passage that borrows from the first refrain at [R24].

Section 9) [R25] Retrograde version of Section 6 transposed a half-step higher. Messiaen complicates the music from the earlier section to produce a retrograde rhythmic canon, now with six rhythmic characters divided into two groups of three characters. The upper group (trumpets and cornet) play in forward motion, while the lower group (horns and trombones) play in retrograde motion. The statue theme is also played as melodic characters by the woodwind/strings and by the piano, and the combination of the three different groups (brass, woodwind/strings, piano) results in harmonic characters that are unrelated to the rhythmic characters but have the same broad aspects of increase, decrease, and no change. Messiaen devotes several pages of the *Traité* to detailed analysis of this section and concludes by noting that he hopes that his explanation will be enough "to give an idea of this jumble of timbres, of harmonies, of rhythms, of the organized disorder of these thousand colors which swirl and interpenetrate, of these intertwined rainbows, of these red flows marbled with green, of these torrents of violet pierced with yellow, these blue oceans starred with orange and furiously rolling their violent and supple waters, of that dynamic, orgiastic, noisy and delirious intoxication like the archetypes of Love and Joy!" (*Traité*: 265).

Section 10) [R32] A return of the ostinato from [R21] of the statue theme as melodic characters. Surrounded by this, the theme of the Refrain goes through the major keys of D (1st period, antecedent); F (1st period, consequent); and D-flat (2nd period shortened and some notes of the 3rd period).

Section 11) [R34] Development of the second verse. A new ostinato bass, in melodic characters, begins here and continues to [R43]. Messiaen alludes to historic precedents and notes that in this last section of the development, as in classical developments, a dominant pedal of the principal key (D-flat major) is implied (*Traité*: 237).

C – Recapitulation
Section 12) [R38] The return of the refrain in D-flat major is presented, with a counterpoint in sixteenth notes in the piano and gamelan as stated at [R6], while the bass ostinato from section 11 continues. The refrain is heard twice and on the second time sticks to the conclusion heard between [R11] and [R12]. Messiaen describes this music as "great cascades of chords" (*Traité*: 238).

Section 13) [R45] The movement ends with a coda that is a "delirium of passion and joy" (*Traité*: 238). A piano cadenza marked "with fire and rage" plays the statue theme in diminution and with a change of register over a quiet roll on the bass drum before the final slow, heavy, loud presentation of the statue theme by the entire ensemble. Messiaen is evocatively descriptive of this coda, noting not only its musical characteristics, but also how the sounds relate to the program:

The perfect D-flat chord finally comes, attacked pianissimo by the tutti, then excessively swollen and long held. It is helped in its crescendo by the trills of metallic percussions (suspended cymbal, Chinese cymbal, tam-tam), and flown over in its formidable final fortissimo by the high-pitched third of the ondes. The Sphinx of Giza (Egypt), the stepped pyramid of the Temple of the Warriors in Chichen Itza (Mexico), better still: some immense and solitary mountain or some terrible abyss, this is what's evoked here – granitic or abyssal – the enormous and heavy thirds of the statue theme! (*Traité*: 273).

Messiaen concludes his analysis by describing the movement as "a nervous, numerous, elaborate tutti, always very dynamic, almost all the time fortissimo" (*Traité*: 272). The effect is breathtaking and was perhaps conceived as a showstopper for the end of the first half of the performance. In the 1990 score, Messiaen notes that, if a performance contains an interval, it should occur here, and adds a footnote that, if there is no interval, there should be a very long silence before the next movement to allow the listener to settle into the luxurious calm of movement 6 (Score: 238).

Movement 6 – *Jardin du sommeil d'amour* [*Garden of love's sleep*] (*très modéré, très tendre* [very moderate, very tender])

Third cyclic theme, or love theme. It is a long and slow melody on the ondes Martenot and the strings, infinitely tender and gentle [suave], ornamented by the vibraphone and the songs of birds in the piano solo. The aerial height of ideal and tender love.

This movement is perhaps one of the most popular single movements Messiaen composed, and by far the most frequently played on streaming services. The evocation of the garden and the birds in the opening minute of the piece establishes an aural ecology that continues with a chorale in the strings and ondes that is lightly decorated with a fascinating range of sounds. Messiaen's program is a beguiling prompt, if the listener chooses that path; but no matter what type of meditational listening one is doing, this is a rich and extraordinary soundscape.

Following the passionate and joyful fifth movement, Messiaen notes the contrast: "That one was carnal, this one is all purity – that one was restless, frantic, this one is calm as sleep – that one was loud, brutal, this one is smooth, tender. Aerial height of the most ideal love" (*Traité*: 275).

Messiaen provides a description of the movement that includes the usual fragmentary reminiscences of the inspirations for the music:

The two lovers are locked in the crystal bubble of Hieronymus Bosch, in the air prison of Viviane and Merlin, in the glass house of Tristan and Isolde, "flowery roses, luminous in the morning when the sun shines."[22] The two lovers are locked in the sleep of love. The two lovers are locked in

---

[22] Bédier, 1924: 266.

Example 9 *Jardin du sommeil d'amour*, mm. 1–7

www.cambridge.org/Shenton

themselves. A landscape emerges from them. The garden around them is called Tristan, the garden which surrounds them is called Isolde. This garden is full of shadows and lights, of plants and of new flowers, of clear and melodious birds which sing of love. "All the birds of the stars" ... "Shortest path from shadow to heaven" (*Harawi*). All the birds and a thousand rustles color the song of love with rainbows. Time passes, forgotten. The lovers [inhabit a place] outside of time. Don't wake them up ... (*Traité*: 275).

The movement is a single long sentence based on the love theme. It is played by muted strings without basses, all of which divide, so that at points the chord is in eight parts. Messiaen requests a true pianissimo and tight vibrato, and colors the sound with the ondes Martenot, which evokes the mystery of the garden by spreading "drops of lunar water after each attack." This timbre Messiaen equates with "distant space," and suggests it "elevates, ennobles, idealizes and surrealizes the entire thing" (*Traité*: 275). The short score (Example 9) shows the gentle counterpoint of the piano, flute, and vibraphone over the chorale.

The song sentence (similar to the song sentences of the two slow movements of the *Quatuor pour la fin du Temps*), is comprised of antecedent and consequent phrases and played in a combination of F-sharp major and mode 2. The long theme represents the lovers, but Messiaen remarks that "There is no garden without flowers, trees, and birds," and explains that "this one is filled with voices, rustles, murmurs," which he describes in detail in the *Traité*. For example, at the start of the movement the piano plays the song of a nightingale with "repeated heavy notes followed by a garland turned towards the treble." Some birds change their songs depending on the season, and here Messiaen places the movement in a very specific time by explaining that the songs he portrays "are typical of the nightingale in love, during the month of May, in the beautiful days and beautiful nights of spring" (*Traité*: 277).

Details of the composition of birdsong on the piano are given in the *Traité*. One of Messiaen's favorite birds, and one that he used frequently, is the blackbird. This song is integrated with the nightingale of the opening and starts one measure before [R1]. Example 10 shows the first of two distinct calls from the blackbird. This one Messiaen describes as "full of gaiety – a sunny, total and communicative gaiety: the little echo at the ending is both a chuckle of pleasure, and a sort of phrase for 'well-done' that the bird awards himself for the beautiful stanza he has just uttered: how well I just sang!" (*Traité*: 286).

Example 10 First blackbird song, piano, one measure before [R1]
www.cambridge.org/Shenton

Messiaen is careful to explain that in *Turangalîla* the birdsongs are not
notated with the accuracy of the ornithologist (as he did in *Réveil des oiseaux*
and especially the *Catalog d'oiseaux*), rather they are "stylized, surrealized,
sublimated – they remain the symbol of the joy of love, in all that it has that is
tender, airy, pure, in all its transcendence of place, hour, space and time"
(*Traité*: 287). In the *Traité* Messiaen describes birds as his friends and as
"those whose idealized song accompanies all my dreams of beauty." This is
followed by brief notes that recall passages in *Harawi* that also include
birdsong, a quote from Éluard, and then a description of birdsong from
Bédier's version of Tristan:

> Tristan knew from childhood the art of counterfeiting the song of the birds of
> the woods; at will, he imitated the oriole, the titmouse, the nightingale and all
> the winged birds; and, sometimes, come to his call, many birds, with swollen
> necks, sang their leaves in the light.
>
> In her room, Isolde was watching. Suddenly, through the half-open window,
> where the rays of the moon were playing, the voice of a nightingale entered.
> Isolde listened to the sonorous voice which came to enchant the night, and the
> voice rose plaintively and in such a way that there is no cruel heart, no
> murderous heart, it would not have moved. The Queen thought: where does
> this melody come from? Suddenly she understood: Ah! it's Tristan! So, in the
> forest of Morois he imitated the songbirds to charm me (*Traité*: 284).

The temple blocks enter around [R4] and are colored by the Turkish cymbal and
the triangle. Messiaen admits that "I like the wooden timbre, the matt timbre, both
poetic and impassive of the temple block." Despite the "apparent coldness" of the
sound, he attributes to it the enigmatic character of the smile of Leonardo da
Vinci's "Mona Lisa," and notes that it "has the exquisite magic of Chinese poetry"
(*Traité*: 281). After describing the mathematical basis of the percussion music at
this point, Messiaen again returns to a summary that moves from a mere description of the mechanics of the music to an explanation of its philosophical aspects,
and includes references to his Tristan Trilogy and also the poetry of Rilke:

> In summary, the two temple blocks follow the same path but in the opposite
> direction, one going towards what was before, towards the past, the other
> going towards what will be after, towards the future. The lovers are sufficient
> in themselves. They are to themselves the future and the past. As it is said of
> love in the fifth *Rechant*, "your eyes travel in the past . . . in the future." Time
> flies like sand in an hourglass. Its quiet gait ascends in a straight line towards
> the future, and simultaneously descends in a retrograde line towards the past.
> The lovers have no consciousness. Their embrace is always present: inces-
> santly transformed into one another, they are almost out of [the boundaries of]
> time. This is the absence of time that we will know after death. The lovers
> (says Rilke) "are very close to it and are astonished." And the double line of

rhythms, forward and retrograde, falls in light drops of water on the orchestral ensemble, made apparent to the listener by all the music and all the divisions of duration that surround it (*Traité*: 281).

In his revisions to the score, Messiaen includes several notations regarding performance practice. For example, at the end of this movement, having moved the listener to a place of quiet contemplation, in the last measure of the piece he requests that the pianist keeps their hands on the keys after the last quiet birdsong phrase until the final chord has ended, thus ensuring minimal physical disruption from the stage. In the *Traité* he also cautions the wood block player, noting that "by allowing themselves [to play] inaccurate rhythms, by inattention or negligence, they distort and destroy the most beautiful image and the most beautiful symbol of my score" (*Traité*: 282).

Messiaen believed that the musical embellishments played over the love theme are an essential part of the music and the experience. With only the long theme in the strings and ondes, the music "would have suppressed all the exquisite rustling of the garden of love, the pretty symbol of time that passes by forgotten by the lovers." This is echoed in Messiaen's final comments on this movement, which summarize both its music and its program: "Le Jardin du sommeil, despite its rustling, rhythms, timbres, and birdsongs, is the great asylum of soft light where lovers sleep, it is a mirror that gives life to all dreams when the sky and the earth are sleeping and that real flowers, real fruit, the true light and the real birds sing in the hearts of lovers their very naked, simple melody crystal, silent as the certainty (*Traité*: 287).

Movement 7 – *Turangalîla II* [Turangalîla 2] (*un peu vif, bien modéré* [a little lively, well moderated])

Again, bird songs in the piano solo, twittering of the Woodwind, a mode of percussive rhythms with chromatic rhythmic values in scattered form. Rhythms like a spreading fan.

To balance the long slow movement, "*Turangalîla 2*" is shorter (the shortest in the entire symphony). It starts with a stylized birdsong on solo piano. This passage is based on the song of the blackbird but modified. Messiaen writes that the blackbird's "offbeat, somewhat mocking character has been preserved," but that elements of the wood warbler can be detected, and that the whole solo is "more strange than joyful" (*Traité*: 289).

At [R1] a melody is played using the technique of *Klangfarbenmelodie*, in which each pitch is assigned to a different instrument, providing a melody that is comprised not only of pitches and rhythms, but also of timbres. Messiaen tried to ensure that the distribution of the pitches and rhythms was distinct from those around it in order to bring it to the attention of the listener, so he divided the line between the gamelan, oboe, clarinet, pizzicato strings, horn, trumpet, alto flute, and others (Ibid.).

The principal musical feature of the second section utilizes his fan technique, representing a fan closing. As an aside, Messiaen alludes to the fact that the technique has been used by other composers and that Rimsky-Korsakov would have called it a "convergent procession" (*Traité*: 290). The "antagonists" in this convergence are the "expressive, almost tender" sound of ondes on one side and the "muddy, thick, sticky depths" of trombones and tuba on the other "which come forward like monstrous dinosaurs" (Ibid.).

The third section begins at [R2] and is primarily based on a rhythmic mode of 16 durations ranging from one sixteenth note to 16 sixteenths. It is played by six percussion instruments, which Messiaen selected based on their ability to be distinguished by the ear (so there are a variety of timbres and pitches). As we would expect, Messiaen complicates the original idea by grouping the instruments and giving each of them a specific ostinato. So, the maracas, Chinese cymbal, and bass drum play the same ostinatos as the triangle, Turkish cymbal, and wood block, but in retrograde order.

At [R3] the fourth section utilizes a technique that Messiaen described as a "jumble" [fouillis] since it consists of multiple melodic lines without any regard for the resulting harmonies. This became more fully developed in his subsequent bird pieces *Réveil des oiseaux* and *Oiseaux exotiques*, and later in the "hors tempo" bird works and reached a pinnacle of perfection in the astounding ninth movement of *Éclairs sur l'au-delà...* titled "Plusieurs oiseaux des arbres de vie." The principal instruments are the oboe and clarinet, which share a melody that Messiaen describes as "Mozartian" (*Traité*: 293). Two of the musical ideas presented here were reused by Messiaen in the *Cinq rechants*. In *Turangalîla II* from [R3] to [R5], a solo cello plays an ostinato with "biting detachment" that Messiaen likens to Hindu music and notes its resemblance to the opening of his fifth *Rechant*. Example 11a shows the cello part at [R3], and Example 11b shows how this became the *Rechant* motif. Messiaen also makes a connection with the cello part in "Danse de la fureur, pour les sept trompettes," the sixth movement of the *Quatuor pour la fin du Temps*, though it is unclear if any extramusical meaning is meant to be conveyed with the music (*Traité*: 294).

Example 11a *Turangalîla*
www.cambridge.org/Shenton

ma-yo-ma ka-li-mo-li-mo ma-yo-ma ka-li-mo-li-mo   Tes yeux vo - ya - gent

Example 11b *Rechant* 5, mm. 1–4
www.cambridge.org/Shenton

(mayoma kalimo [untranslatable] your eyes travel)

The fifth section of this movement is a retrograde of the music in section 2 ([R1] to [R2]). It is followed by what Messiaen describes as one of the most rhythmically complex in the entire symphony. The main theme of this sixth section is given to metallic instruments (small Turkish cymbal, suspended cymbal, Chinese cymbal, tam-tam) with two rhythmic characters that, like *Turangalîla I*, has one that increases and one that decreases. The rest of the orchestra utilizes the chord theme in four registers: high, low, medium, and very low, which are assigned different timbres. The focal point of this section is the tam-tam between [R7] and [R9], which Messiaen said should be "very powerful, very violent," and which he describes as "like an endlessly renewed abyss, more and more black, more and more deep, more and more terrible" (*Traité*: 297). He elaborates on the programmatic element, stating: "The opposition between the decrease and the increase, between the narrowing and the widening of the two perpetually alternating rhythmic characters, recalls the double horror of the reddened iron wall which tightens and of the unspeakable, of the unspeakable depth of the well tortures, in the famous tale of Edgar Allan Poe's *The Pit and the Pendulum*" (Ibid.).

The music that follows utilizes a series of chromatic durations on the triangle and bass drum. The snare drum has three iterations of a rhythm that uses the third Greek epitrite (long, long, short, long), and the vibraphone repeats music from section 4; however, this time the ondes works in a melodic and rhythmic canon with it. The piano supplies a rhythmic canon pedal, using the rhythm shown in Example 12.

Example 12 Piano, rhythmic canon pedal at [R7]
www.cambridge.org/Shenton

This rhythm is comprised of the three deçî-tâlas, which Messiaen has utilized in combination elsewhere in the piece: râgavardhana, candrakalâ, and lakskmîça. The piano uses three chords to express these rhythms, which Messiaen reused from the movement "Syllables" in *Harawi*. Again, it is not clear if any of the content of the poem of this movement is implied along with the music, but it is a moot point to the average listener who would not be expected to reference the borrowed music. Here Messiaen utilizes again the alchemists' technique "to dissociate and coagulate" (*Traité*: 301).

The seventh section [R9] briefly reprises the piano birdsong from the opening, which is developed and combined with the statue theme before a tam-tam roll leads into a short coda. The final measures combine the *Klangfarbenmelodies* from [R1] and [R6], and the movement ends with a repeat of the brief piano motif that ends the opening cadenza and a short hit on the bass drum.

Movement 8 – *Développement de l'amour* [Development of love] (*bien modéré* [well moderated])

> *Besides a canon in nonreversible rhythms, and lyric offshoots of the love theme, this part develops the three cyclic themes with a passion that is constantly increasing.*

The last of the four love movements continues from the point where the lovers have become one in the timeless space of the garden. Messiaen acknowledges that "This formidable title immediately suggests that this is about an increased love, with an ever-growing passion, a creative passion which multiplies itself *ad infinitum*, a love in which the ever-new moments overlap each other in a surreal and magical becoming, piling immortal pasts on sunny futures, with a gigantic, living love, like the waves of the sea. And it is true. Like the Tristan and Isolde of the Middle Ages, they will never be able to let go: the love potion has forever linked them" (*Traité*: 309).

Messiaen also notes that the title is a play on words and that, although there has been rhythmic development throughout the symphony, this is the movement that contains musical development beyond the rhythmic. The movement is in three main sections, a short introduction, a "grand development" that includes the climax of the entire symphony, and a short coda.

A) Introduction

The principal rhythmic feature at the start of the introduction section is a nonretrogradable rhythm, for which each value decreases at each repeat by

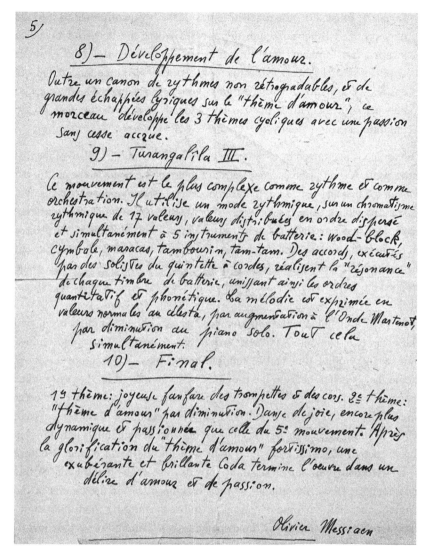

Figure 15 Messiaen's BSO program note for movements 8 to 10

a sixteenth note. The piano part is based on the chord theme (heard previously in movements 2 and 7, and repeated in the final movement) using a repeating rhythmic pattern: ♩ ♩ ♩ ♪. For Messiaen, this music "creates a painful feeling of insecurity," which causes us to "float between two times of life, between two spaces of death." He explains this with reference again to the main programmatic elements:

Whether she is called Isolde, brewer of potions; or Viviane and her air prison, or whether she has dominated death by the power of her will like the

Ligeia of Edgar Poe, the magical forces of the lover introduce us into the
dark room of Bluebeard, into the abysses where the beautiful Eurydice
awaited her Orpheus, and sing like my *Cinq rechants*: "the explorer
Orpheus finds its heart in death." Like Pélleas in the cellars of the old
castle, we are seized with vertigo – vertigo on a higher scale, vertigo
between heaven and earth, vertigo of death and love, the fear of the
unfathomable and the mystery (*Traité:* 312).

The vertigo is interrupted by a "waterfall" (similar to the music at [R6] of the first
movement). A short piano cadenza leads to a return of the statue theme at [R6] but
without the first and last chord, followed by a succession of eight chords heard at
[R5] and previously in the first movement. For Messiaen, this is fearful and terrifying
music. He equates the statue theme here to the Vénus d'Ille of Mérimée, "the giant of
bronze hugging her lover and smothering him in her hard arms. On this last blow of
the tam-tam, the lover is dead, Venus killed him, and, as Mérimée says: 'the statue
dropped the corpse and went out.' Nothing remains but a pit of shadow" (*Traité*:
317).

At [R2] a chamber ensemble comprising two oboes, English horn, two
clarinets, two bassoons, 1st and 3rd horns, a cornet, four first violins,
four second violins, four violas, and four cellos, plays a version of the chord
theme that is different from the previous iteration played in "heavy bundles
[paquets]" by the piano. The new version is scattered, spread out in different
timbres in a sort of *klangfarbenakkord*. This is a technique Messiaen devised,
which he describes using the doctrinal formula of the alchemists noted for his
fourth theme, in which something is broken into its basic elements before
being reformed into something new. In this case (and in the coda of this
movement at [R46]) he alludes to the breaking down of the chords in the
single timbre and dynamic of the piano and reconstituting them into something that sounds entirely new by dispersing them among the various instruments and utilizing the inherent dynamics of the subsections of the orchestra
(*Traité*: 312, 324).[23]

B) Grand development

The development section occupies most of the movement (from [R8] to [R46]).
Messiaen divides it into eleven sections, the most important of which are the
three "explosions" of the love theme, which represent increasingly passionate
eruptions of the musical and programmatic ideas.

---

[23] See also *Traité*: 301, where Messiaen describes its use in *Turangalîla 2*.

a) [R8] Motif A (a new theme) in F-sharp major, measures 12 and 13 of the love theme in E-flat major, the chord theme in the piano. [R10] the flower theme on clarinets accompanied by a rapid trill by the ondes. Messiaen describes the trill as a "lunar halo of mystery and beyond," and ventures an unusual moment of self-doubt regarding the orchestration as he wonders: "Maybe I was wrong to repeat this effect for each reprise of the flower theme in the eighth movement? It is very surprising, [perhaps] too surprising, and, in the long run, the surprise dulls" (*Traité*: 318).

b) [R11] A parallel to section a). Motif A in G major, measures 12 and 13 of the love theme in E major. Flower theme on clarinets with the metallic trill of the ondes. Ascending figures in the strings and descending figures in the wind and basses coupled with an extreme rallentando prepare for the ecstatic outburst of the next section.

c) [R15] First explosion of the love theme, fortissimo, from the beginning of its second section from its appearance at [R4] in the sixth movement. Here Messiaen makes a specific allusion to the famous Liebestod from Wagner's opera *Tristan und Isolde* (Act 3, measure 1681 onwards) in the trumpet, strings, and ondes. Messiaen's melody and harmony are strikingly similar to Wagner's, and, given the underlying themes both pieces share, this is the perfect opportunity for Messiaen to pay homage to the earlier work.

d) [R16] Passionate motif B (a second new theme), which Messiaen also describes as "terrifying," includes a violin glissando "whistling like a storm wind ... descending from the wave that cries above the raging elements" (*Traité*: 319). Against this, a retrograde rhythmic canon plays between woodwind and trombones.

e) [R18] A parallel to sections a) and b). Motif A in A-flat major, measures 12 and 13 of the love theme in F major. Flower theme on clarinets.

f) [R21] A parallel to section e). Motif A in A major, chord theme in the piano, measures 12 and 13 of the love theme in E-flat major. Flower theme on clarinets.

g) [R27] Second explosion of the love theme, fortissimo, in D major. Here, however, instead of starting the love theme at its second section, the entire antecedent phrase is also played, and this intensifies the effect.

h) [R29] Motif A in F-sharp major, with the chord theme and constant inter-polations of the passionate motive B. A repeat of the retrograde rhythmic canon between woodwind and trombones from [R17].

i) [R32] A parallel to section h). Motif A in G major, again with constant interpolations of the B motive. Another repeat of the retrograde rhythmic canon between woodwind and trombones, but this time a tone higher.

j) To [R35], repeat of the last three chords of motif A in B-flat, in D, and in F-sharp are part of the preparation in this section for the last great explosion of love ("which will be the most terrifying by far"). Motif B is reintroduced, and the music surges towards the climax.

k) [R42] A third explosion of the love theme, in F-sharp major, the loudest and the longest of all. For Messiaen, this is the climax of the entire symphony, and he describes its music and effect in detail, comparing it to the death scenes of Isolde and Brünhilde in Wagner's operas. The music depicts the total union of two lovers, which is love's ultimate goal: "it is no longer such a man and such a woman, it is Tristan-Isolde only with deletion of the word 'and,' it is love grown in a mythical state, it is a reflection of Eternal Love. It is these 'flowers which open infinitely, this pure unsupervised [air] that we breathe,' of which Rilke speaks in *The Duino Elegies*, which only lovers understand (as well as children and the dying)." Messiaen also describes this moment, citing the painting by surrealist artist Roland Penrose titled *Seeing is believing* (or *L'ille invisible*), which was also the inspiration for movement 10 of *Harawi*, "Amor oiseau d'étoile." In the painting "an upturned head of a woman begins with the hair at the bottom of the table, continues through the forehead, eyes, face, neck . . . then emerges on the sky and on the stars." Messiaen quotes his own text for *Harawi*, which describes the painting:

> All the birds of the stars,
> Far from the picture my hands are singing,
> Star, increased silence of the sky,
> My hands, your eye, your neck, the sky.

The moment is played pianissimo in *Harawi*, fortissimo in *Turangalîla*, but the meaning is the same: "Tristan and Isolde are transcended by Tristan-Isolde, in a higher Love, archetype of all loves" (*Traité*: 321).

C) Coda

[R46] The coda is a varied reprise of the introduction. The nonretrogradable rhythm is the same as at the beginning, enriched with a triple rhythmic canon based on the statue theme between three groups: 1) trumpets and horns, 2) trombones and tuba, and 3) bells and metallic percussion. Messiaen describes the combination of all these elements as "a jumble as dense, as tangled as the complicated vaults, the dark stairs of Piranesi, the interweaving of branches and foliage, the inextricable knots of female hair and water whirlpools by Leonardo da Vinci. Trumpets and trombones emerge from this cataclysm, like the giant Asuras of Hindu mythology, like evil mountains, overwhelming and relentless" (*Traité*: 326).

Two measures before [R49], the horn glissando is repeated from the introduction. The waterfall music is removed, but the short piano cadenza is repeated in the opposite direction. The movement closes with a grand statement based on the statue theme. It ends with a huge strike on the tam-tam, which replaces the seventh note of the theme and is colored by a low cluster in the piano, a bass pizzicato note, and a trill on the bass drum. Messiaen describes this again as terrifying and describes the frightening image he wished to conjure to end the movement:

> A dreadful abyss opens – we think of the nameless horrors of *The Pit and the Pendulum* of Poe, the explorer Orpheus and the lover of the *Vénus d'Ille* who found their heart in death, the pit of torture offers a look at all the terror, all the vertigo of its darkest and most secret cavities, the echoes of the caves underground vibrate in our ears, constructing the languages of the afterlife – and the statue leans above the abyss (*Traité*: 331).

Movement 9 – *Turangalîla III* [Turangalîla 3] (*bien modéré* [well moderated])

This movement is the most complex in rhythm and in orchestration. It makes use of a mode on a rhythmic chromaticism of seventeen values, values distributed in dispersed order simultaneously by five percussion instruments: wood block, cymbal, maracas, tambourine, tam-tam. Chords played by the quintet of solo strings create the "resonance" of each percussive timbre; thus unifying the quantitative and phonetic elements. The melody is expressed in normal values by the celesta, in augmentation by the ondes Martenot, and in diminution by the piano solo. All of this happens simultaneously.

After a short opening melody on clarinet (colored and elaborated by a few instruments including the ondes and vibraphone), a rhythmic mode begins at [R2]. It is comprised of 17 chromatic durations (ranging from a sixteenth note value to a value of 17 sixteenth notes), which are ordered normally and by superimposition and noted as such in the 1990 score. Messiaen assigns this to several percussion instruments and notes the different sound each makes (with the sequence of numbers of sixteenth notes marked in square brackets): wood block (clear, high) [4, 5, 7, 3, 2, 1, 6, 17, 14], suspended cymbal (medium, metallic, resonant scrambled) [11, 13], maracas (dry, sneezed) [15, 12, 16, 10, 9, 8], Provencal tambourine (dull and heavy) [14, 17, 6, 1, 2, 3, 7, 5, 4] – the reverse of the wood block, and finally tam-tam (bass, very prolonged resonance) [8, 9, 10, 16, 12, 15]. The tambourine values are the reverse (retrograde canon) of the wood block, and the tam-tam values the reverse of the maracas. This theme is then taken up by the gamelan instruments and piano with a *klangfarbenmelodie* that Messiaen describes as "less varied, but more incisive, more powerful than before" (*Traité*: 334).

At [R3] Messiaen notes in the score that there is a reversal of music by timbre so that the durations in the wood block pass to the tam-tam and those of the cymbal to the tambourine, while the maracas play the same durations as before. For the remainder of the movement, this rhythmic mode is the foundational musical material. It is repeated with successive additions expressed before each duration: first, a sixteenth note expressed before each duration; second, two sixteenth notes expressed before each duration; and third, a trill with a duration of five sixteenth notes before each duration. As before, each set of the new 17 rhythms are dispersed and superimposed, and then immediately repeated with reversal of durations and timbres. In order to escape from this mathematical device and end the movement, once the third set is over each instrument trills continuously until the last note of the piece.

Starting at [R5] a group of 13 muted strings (with the disposition 2/4/3/2/2) begin to play a series of "soft and mysterious" chords that are derived from the resonances of the percussion instruments. Each of the five sets of string instruments plays the rhythm of one of the five percussion instruments using chords of 2, 3, or 4 pitches derived from five different modes of limited transposition, each with their own specific color. This is an advance on the usual color associations for Messiaen. He explains as follows:

> Each mode color matches the tone and attack color of the percussion instrument chosen, and one hears, not two colors, but a single new color, resulting from the alloy, which reinforces the durations and makes the hearing more poetic and more appreciable. Harmony is rhythmic, the rhythm is colored with chords, the quantitative order (durations) and the phonetic order (attacks, timbres, colors) are linked to one another, and their marriage transforms them into a single sonorous flesh that could respond to names made up of variously expressive terms: harmonies-attacks, numbers-colors, timbres-durations (*Traité*: 360).

Even though it is comparatively short, the music in this penultimate movement is so complicated and intense that Messiaen notes in the revised score that there should be a long silence before the final movement is played (Score: 363).

Movement 10 – *Final* [Finale] *(modéré, presque vif, avec une grande joie* [moderate, almost lively, with great joy])

First theme: a joyous fanfare on trumpets and horns. Second theme: love theme in diminution. Dance of joy, more dynamic and impassioned than that of the fifth movement. After the glorification of the love theme [played] fortissimo, an exuberant and brilliant coda ends the work in a delirium of love and passion.

Messiaen's summary of the form divides the final movement into nine sections:

1. The first theme (a new one) is presented as a fanfare in F-sharp major.

2. At [R3] a very short bridge passage.
3. At [R4] the second theme (which is the love theme, but in rapid movement in diminution and in E-flat major).
4. At [R6] the development, which is in five sections:

   a) The opening theme (combined with the chord theme): in G, then in A-flat, then in A. The opening theme is reduced to howling notes with repeated fortissimo chords.

   b) At [R11] the second theme in F, at [R12] the second theme in A-flat, and at [R13] a short development of the second theme.

   c) At [R14] the movement's first theme in D major combined with the chord theme (which is modified by changes of timbres and registers).

   d) At [R15] the first theme (combined with the chord theme) in B, then in C major, then in opposite movement. The first theme is reduced to two notes, crying, howling, with thunderous chords repeated fortissimo.

   e) At [R20], after a climax at the end of the first theme (with a bass ostinato in asymmetric enlargement), the music ends in the dominant of the movement's principal key.

5. At [R24] the first theme returns in F-sharp major (in a varied presentation using counterpoints of chords in ascending and descending scales). The music proceeds to the second theme without a bridge passage.
6. At [R27] the second theme returns, also in F-sharp major.
7. At [R29] there is a development of the second part of the love theme (still in rapid movement, in diminution). Cascade of chords, a huge crescendo, and an enormous rallentando lead to:
8. At [R34] the love theme, at its correct (true) tempo, very slow, in tutti fortissimo, forming a large augmentation of the second theme of the movement. This apotheosis of glory and joy is the climax of the movement and the final climax of the whole symphony. Messiaen describes it as a "never-ending joy," so it remains in the dominant, and is followed by:
9. At [R36] a coda based on the opening (head) of the first theme.

Messiaen provides a detailed description of the first theme, which is a fanfare for the entire ensemble. The music is derived in part from the meters of classical Greek and Latin poetry. The opening of the first theme is glyconic, having the rhythm [– u | – u u | – u | –] (where – is long and u is short). Messiaen changes the accentuation so that it does not sound as a glyconic, but instead is accentuated like a choriambe [– u u –] where the second short rhythm is accented. This part of the opening theme is 13 sixteenth notes long and is balanced by a phrase that is 14 sixteenth notes played in steady sixteenths until the final chord (see Example 13).

Example 13 Fanfare theme
www.cambridge.org/Shenton

As a rhythmic counterpoint to the first theme, an ostinato is played on the wood block and Turkish cymbal, which juxtaposes three deçî-tâlas Messiaen has utilized throughout the symphony: râgavardhana in retrograde by augmentation, candrakalâ by diminution, and lakskmîça by augmentation.

For the return of the love theme (at [R4]), the music is not slow as it was in movements 6 and 8. Here it is in a faster tempo, and Messiaen describes the music by analogy with the paintings of Chagall and with quotations from his own text for movement 1 of *Cinq rechants*:

> The rapid, light love theme, by reduction, is the illustration of this going beyond, so well-marked in the paintings of Marc Chagall, where lovers fly away: they have their own myth, and their aerial joy overcame the laws of gravity: here they are gone above the clouds to the search for new planets: the protective fairy blew on them, they flew away like birds. "Lovers fly away / Brangien, in space you blow / lovers fly away / towards the stars of death" (*Traité*: 372).

The five parts of the development section principally utilize the chord theme [R6, R14], and the love theme [R12], subjected to various mathematical procedures already seen in the symphony. At [R24] the movement's first theme is reprised, and at [R27] the second theme is reprised. These morph into a long cascade of chords divided between sections of the orchestra and each in different modes. This is all preparatory for the climax of this movement.

As Messiaen notes, the apotheosis of the love theme comes at [R34] presented in its true tempo (as in movement 6), but here played fortissimo by the entire orchestra (without percussion) and "crowned by the supraterrestrial voice of the ondes which dominates the tutti." To provide a musically satisfying end to both the movement and entire symphony, Messiaen utilizes a traditional dominant to tonic cadence wrapped in his own musical language. One measure before [R36], the melody stops on the penultimate note (a G-sharp belonging to the dominant 7th chord [second inversion]), which is played with a fortissimo crescendo. Messiaen describes this point as being "in a state of tension, of luminous expectation, of unfulfilled sensitive body – and this great gesture towards an end which does not exist (Glory and Joy are endless), attracts and provokes the coda" (*Traité*: 382).

The coda reuses the opening of the fanfare theme, the chord theme, and the theme of love. All of these have strong impetus to the final F-sharp major chord, crowned by the ondes, which has a series of ascending trills "as a jubilant lark soars to the sun." From [R36], the bells repeat a chime "which increases the tutti's rainbow of joy," while "a waterfall of chords on Woodwind and strings then on tutti" play a series of pitches derived from the bridge passage at [R3]. Messiaen's description of the music captures the excitement of the various elements combined:

> All these colors: these reds and these blues, these yellow and purple mauve, these bluish green and darker purple, these coppers and golds, these sapphire and Chartres blues, these purple magenta mixed with orange red, these light coffee mixed with reddish brown, these purples striped with yellow, with the red of the trumpets and the leaden gray of the massive and rapid descent of the trombones and tuba: all this whirling falls on the notes C-sharp and F-sharp, hammered in the extreme bass by the piano solo, to which the fortissimo bass drum adds the brutality of its cannon shots (*Traité*: 384).

Part of the excitement of the coda comes from its compressed time frame: just 60 measures from [R36] to the end. The surge toward the final cadence starts at [R39] and brings the work to a powerful close:

> For the second time, and with a rise in successive trills which are longer and start from below, the ondes rushes towards the heights. The bells still cry out their rainbow of joy. The suspended cymbal trill swells more and more, and the maelstrom of light and glory ends with the first four notes of the first theme, one last time shouted in tutti fortissimo, in the sparkling diamonds of F-sharp major and the powerful surge of metallic percussion rolls (*Traité*: 384).

6 1990 Revisions to the Score

In his program note to the recording conducted by Myung-Whun Chung (issued in 1991, but recorded in 1990), Messiaen noted that he was working with Durand to publish a revised version of the symphony that contains "some small changes that have been suggested to me by my hearing around two hundred performances of the work." Messiaen made the changes in 1990 (which were added to the original engraved plates). Making changes to the score was not his usual practice, so perhaps it shows some of the special feeling he had for the piece.

The changes to the prefatory material are largely practical and derived from experience. For example, the estimated duration of the piece is changed from

1 hour 15 minutes to 1 hour 25 minutes (while the *Traité* analysis lists 1 hour 20 minutes [*Traité*: 151]). The suggestion about possible separate performance of a single movement or movements is removed, and Messiaen asserts that the work was conceived as a whole and should be played without interruption (but concedes that, if there is to be an interval, it should be between movements 5 and 6, which is how it was performed at the premiere).

The revised instrument list includes information about the notation of the vibraphone part in the "keyboard" section and moves the eight tubular bells out of the section labeled "batterie" (now renamed "percussions" and containing only unpitched instruments) to the keyboard section, where it is labeled "Jeu de Cloches – tubes." This page also contains two notes in the revised score. The first advocates for placement of the piano and ondes Martenot at the front of the stage with the piano at the left of the conductor and the ondes at the right. This may have been for visual aesthetics or for sound balance, but it may also have been to underscore the notion that these two instruments are virtuoso solo parts (confirmed by the solo billing afforded to the players of these instruments). The second note confirms that the glockenspiel part is played with mallets or with a keyed glockenspiel (jeu de timbres). In addition, page (viii) of the 1990 score elaborates on the brief notes on page (v) regarding the glockenspiel part in case a keyed glockenspiel is unavailable and makes a suggestion about rescoring if the vibraphone has a limited range.

The percussion section is large and important to the work, so it is important to be precise about who plays what. In the original score Messiaen notes that the fourteen instruments are divided between five players. In the 1990 edition Messiaen lists only the unpitched percussion (having moved the pitched percussion to the keyboard section) and uses a scheme devised by French percussionist Gérard Pérotin, who rationalized the process. The new scheme divides the instruments into four groups (labeled A, B, C, and D) and requires eight players, not five. A diagram shows the disposition of the instruments and the players and is followed by a detailed description of which instruments are used in each movement.

In the 41 years between the two versions of the score, the symphony was performed many times, so the revised score updates the one-page list of "first performances" with a nine-page list of performances from the world premiere in 1949 up to 1993 (because, although the revisions were made in 1990, the score was not published until 1994).

Revisions in the score itself include extensive and significant alterations to metronome markings, as well as alterations and additions to verbal tempo markings, dynamics, and expression markings. For example, on p. 238 there is modification of both the tempo and metronome markings from "Heavy, more slowly, (dotted eighth-note = 80)" to "Heavy, slow, (dotted eighth-note = 60)." Other details added to the 1990 score include pedal markings to the piano part and clarification of performance instructions. For example, on p. 240 of the first edition, the vibraphone is marked as sounding an octave higher; however, in the second edition this has been removed and a note added that states "throughout this movement, as an exception, the vibraphone part is written at sounding pitch."

In a few cases, idiosyncratic expression markings have been removed. For example, in movement 8 the first edition has the direction "carnal and terrible" on pages 296, 309, and 313, which have been removed in the later edition. This is probably because those terms are descriptions of the music rather than directions on how to play it, whereas in each place Messiaen left the direction "with passion."

Messiaen was evidently not happy with issues of balance, so he adjusted the number of solo string players in places (see, for example, p. 129, which adjusts dynamic markings and the number of players to reinforce different musical lines and pitches) and added footnotes to clarify his intentions. On pages 17, 19, and 29, for example, he notes that "one should hear the second violins and violas" during a passage that also includes woodwind, brass, percussion, and piano. He also highlights some small details that performers had presumably consistently overlooked, such as the footnote on p. 124, which instructs the woodwind and horns to carefully observe an accented note placed on an unaccented rhythm.

He also added footnotes to draw attention to musical devices in the score in order to make them more prominent for the attention of the conductor (and, in turn, the players). This includes noting appearances of the cyclic themes (see, for example, p. 3, where the first theme is noted). Other additions point to both musical devices and the prominence they should receive. For example, on p. 99 a footnote highlights the rhythmic devices, noting: "One must hear the maracas, wood block and bass drum which form three 'rhythmic characters.' The maracas decrease, the bass drum increases, the wood block stays the same. The numbers [written into the score above each pitch] indicate the number of sixteenth notes for each character."

The additions are all improvements by the composer, so the earlier score is now really only of historical interest and performers, and those studying the score should utilize the later version.

7 Reception History and Interpretation

Despite its initial mixed reviews, the symphony has retained a place in the concert hall and in recordings. Messiaen notes there were more than 200 performances during his lifetime; however, updated information on the exact number of performances is not available from the publisher Durand. Internet searches reveal many instances of performances by orchestras around the world, including 13 performances at the BBC Proms since 1969, and 18 by the Boston Symphony Orchestra.[24]

In June 2022, Discogs.com listed 181 "classical" entries for the symphony, though there are duplications because recordings have been reedited and reissued and, occasionally, excerpted (especially movement 6).[25] YouTube has hundreds of videos for the piece, including dozens of complete performances. These recordings and performances include many in which Messiaen was directly or indirectly involved and which bear what musicologist John Milsom describes as a "manner of realization" for his music based on Messiaen's preferences that were communicated during rehearsals but are not contained in the original score.[26] The earliest commercial recording at which the composer was present was recorded in Paris on October 11 and 13, 1961, and released the following year on the Véga label. The Orchestre National de la RTF was conducted by Maurice Le Roux with Yvonne and Jeanne Loriod as the piano and ondes soloists. The recording included an interview with Messiaen and Claude Samuel, taped on November 23, 1961 (Hill and Simeone, 2005: 242).

Although he did a creditable job of the premiere, Bernstein never conducted *Turangalîla* again; however, recordings of some of the rehearsals for the premiere were remastered using 24-bit digital technology and released as part of a box set in celebration of Symphony Hall's centennial in 2001.[27]

Many notable Messiaen interpreters have made commercial recordings of the work, so listeners have a wide choice, depending on their preference for performers. The following are a representative selection of the most acclaimed interpretations on record (orchestra/conductor/pianist/ondist/year):

London Symphony Orchestra/André Previn/Michel Béroff/Jeanne Loriod/1978
Philharmonia Orchestra/Esa-Pekka Salonen/Paul Crossley/Tristan Murail/1986

---

[24] www.bbc.co.uk/proms/events/works/ec48e2cb-8e50-4648-89ba-ec86fb914304, https://archives.bso.org.

[25] Interestingly, Discogs lists several tracks with the title Turangalîla from artists as diverse as Clara Mondshine (aka EDM artist Walter Bachauer), and the Scott Colley Jazz Quartet, though from a search of these artists online it is not clear if they derive any inspiration from Messiaen's work.

[26] Milsom, 1995: 60. For a discussion of some of the issues of Messiaen's recordings and the concept of a "manner of realization," see Shenton, 2007.

[27] www.discogs.com/release/13213761-Boston-Symphony-Orchestra-Symphony-Hall-Centennial-Celebration.

Orchestre de la Bastille/Myung-Wun Chung/Yvonne Loriod/Jeanne Loriod/ 1991

Royal Concertgebouw Orchestra/Riccardo Chailly/Jean-Yves Thibaudet/ Takashi Harada/1993

Tonkünster-Orchester/Yutaka Sado/Roger Muraro/Valerie Hartmann-Claverie/ 2018

Nationaltheater-Orchestra Mannheim/Alexander Soddy/Tamara Stefanovich/ Thomas Bloch/2020

Messiaen was not aware of the technological advances that now allow for recordings to be easily available to consumers via streaming services. Although owning a recording in any format does not force a listener to hear a work from start to finish, the availability of data from streaming services does reveal that people are, in general, not listening to the whole symphony in one sitting. On June 1, 2022, Spotify Premium in the US listed nineteen full recordings of the piece. This would suggest that there should be 190 track listings; however, there are actually 378 separate track listings because some recordings were reissued and are listed under each issue, and some, such as the radio recording of the European premiere in 1950, include additional information like the announcements and introduction from the original broadcast. The 1991 Deutsche Grammaphon recording is by far the most popular, but the number of times each track has been played is revealing. As of June 1, 2022, the first movement has been played 105,667 times. The movement that had been listened to least was movement 8, "Développement de l'amour," with just 47,902 plays. The intense slow movement "Jardin du sommeil d'amour" had been played an astonishing 1,891,738 times, almost forty times the number of plays of movement 8.

A Definitive Recording

Messiaen worked extensively with Myung-Whun Chung on a recording issued by Deutsche Grammaphon (DG 431-781-2). The work was recorded in Paris at the Opéra de Paris-Bastille in October 1990 and issued the following year. Chung conducted the Orchestre De L'Opéra Bastille with Yvonne and Jeanne Loriod as the soloists. Messiaen enthusiastically endorsed the recording, noting that the performance includes all the changes he made to the score, confirming that "These are the correct tempos, the correct dynamics, the right feelings and the right joy!" He commends the recording, saying that "Coming after the many excellent interpretations that we already know, this new version, superb from every point of view, can be considered henceforth the definitive account." Messiaen was often enthusiastic in his endorsement of recordings. For example, he describes the organ recordings by Jennifer Bate as "truly perfect"; however, this, of course, does not preclude other performances from being good, since the composer's opinion is not necessarily the arbiter of taste and there have been many performances that Messiaen never heard.

By comparison, a recording of a live performance from January 29, 1959, conducted by Manuel Rosenthal with the Loriods as soloists and the "definitive" Deutsche Grammaphon recording show that, in general, the preference moved to more expansive performances, since eight of the ten movements are longer in the second version. This is particularly the case for the slow movement "Jardin du sommeil d'amour" which is more than 30 percent slower in the 1991 recording.

Movement	Live 1959	DG 1991[28]
1. Introduction	5:59	6:25
2. Chant d'amour 1	7:57	8:14
3. Turangalîla 1	4:63	5:26
4. Chant d'amour 2	11:46	11:03
5. Joie du sang des étoiles	6:13	6:42
6. Jardin du sommeil d'amour	8:51	12:39
7. Turangalîla 2	4:00	4:11
8. Développement d'amour	10:58	11:41
9. Turangalîla 3	4:49	4:27
10. Final	6:36	7:44

Visual Accompaniment and Ballet Versions

Technological advances and changes in audiences' taste in the early twenty-first century have resulted in more frequent use of visual presentations paired with orchestral music. This would be useful for *Turangalîla*, since much of what Messiaen wrote in the score could be explained using synchronous visuals that indicate through words and images what Messiaen conceived and where he placed it. Images of the birds that are "singing" in the music, for example, along with strategic markers such as the cyclic themes, changes in sections, and even some of the more complex musical devices would help the audience interpret and decipher the music. Even this could not fully detail in a synchronous presentation the enormous complexity of the piece. It would be possible, however, to connect a preconcert lecture with synchronous visuals that are

---

[28] The timings for the 1959 recording are taken from the 2014 Ina reissue on Spotify; those for the 1991 Deutsche Grammaphon recording are from the liner notes and may include a few seconds of silence before and after each track.

elucidating. To date, no one has done this for *Turangalîla*; however, limited use of artwork (including images by one of Messiaen's favorite painters, Robert Delauney) was employed during a performance by the St. Louis Symphony Orchestra conducted by David Robertson at Carnegie Hall on February 15, 2008.[29]

Despite the size of the orchestra (which makes it expensive to perform) and the complexity of the music (which makes it hard to choreograph), *Turangalîla* has been staged as a ballet on several occasions. The first person to suggest this to Messiaen was a French tax official, Hubert Devillez.[30] At a meeting in 1952, the project was discussed with a group that included composers Jacques Ibert and Darius Milhaud, artist Marc Chagall, and the director of the Opéra de Paris, Maurice Lehmann. Two potential choreographers were being considered at that time, Serge Lifar and Léonide Massine. According to Simeone, "Devillez's outline for *Turangalîla* was dropped by the Opéra on the grounds that it was too lurid and erotic" (Simeone, 2007: 291).

As noted earlier, Messiaen did, at one stage, approve a modified performance of the symphony that included just three movements: Turangalîla 1, Chant d'amour 2, and Joie du sang des étoiles. A ballet using this version was choreographed by Peter van Dijk and premiered at the Hamburg Opera on June 22, 1960. The movements were renamed, and the program indicates that the first two were duets and the third a duet but also included the State Opera Ballet (Ibid: 292):

1. Solitude   Erica Lihn, Heinze Schmiedel
2. Chant d'amour   Christa Kempf, Heinz Clauss
3. Danse Joyeuse   Jacqueline Royet, Peter van Dijk and the company

Messiaen did not attend, and, although ideas for a *Turangalîla* ballet continued to crop up periodically, it wasn't until 1967 that the idea for a ballet at the Paris Opéra was seriously back in discussion. This time the proposal had the support of composer Georges Auric and choreographer Roland Petit. Artist Max Ernst was brought on for stage and costume design, and the conductor was Manuel Rosenthal. The première on June 12, 1968 (with Yvonne and Jeanne Loriod reprising their roles as pianist and ondist), was a great success.[31] Petit's program notes describe the work as "a ballet without a story," and "a great wave of love, and a quest for the absolute, which can only be reached after death." His

---

[29] www.gettyimages.com/photos/david-robertson-conductor.

[30] For more details on Messiaen and ballet, and the *Turangalîla* projects, see Simeone, 2007.

[31] For images of the ballet see
www.granger.com/results.asp?inline=true&image=0795335&wwwflag=1&itemx=12 and
www.gettyimages.com/photos/%22turangalila%22.

notes also offered a brief description of the entire concept, which borrows and extends ideas from Messiaen himself:

> The ballet comprises ten movements: the birth of the hero, temptations, the elements, the meeting of the ideal woman, the wedding, sleep, the forces of evil symbolized by a grouping of people which recalls the monsters in Hieronymus Bosch, the death of the lovers (which I wanted to have as little lyricism as possible), the procession of the mourners, and the resurrection. No stories, and choreography which is "horizontal" – more slid than danced, with the dancers often lying on the stage, evoking some movements from Far Eastern dances. . . . I took my inspiration from a quotation by Paul Valéry: "From forms derived from movements, there is a transition to movements derived from forms, through a simple variation of duration." I have chosen to choreograph the work this way, since it seems to correspond most closely to the great symphony of love which is *Turangalîla*. Despite this style "level with the ground," *Turangalîla* is a classical ballet (Ibid: 297).

The ballet was only performed once. Hubert Devillez, the man who first proposed the possibility of a *Turangalîla* ballet but was not involved with the 1968 performance, sued Messiaen and won a financial reward for his "joint work" on the project (Ibid: 298).

A new ballet version was devised by John Neumeier for the Hamburg Ballet in 2016, with Kent Nagano conducting the Philharmonic State Orchestra Hamburg. Neumeier is also credited with the lighting design, while sets were by Heinrich Tröger and costumes by Albert Kriemler.[32] Neumeier's version was revived in 2021 at the Festspielhaus Baden-Baden, with the SWR Symphonieorchester conducted by Maxime Pascal. Publicity material declares that "Neumeier has created a choreography that largely dispenses with narrative and celebrates pure dance: from the grand pas de deux to classical tours en l'air, in which the dancers leap and spin out of pure joie de vivre."[33] A smaller-scale production was created by choreographer Andrew McNicol for The New York Choreographic Institute in 2017.[34]

Use in Film

IMDb does not indicate if music from *Turangalîla* has been used in any movies, though it does list two documentaries about the piece: an 18-minute French documentary in black and white, which includes rehearsals for a performance

---

[32] www.hamburgballett.de/en/schedule/play–repertoire.php?SNr=676. For a teaser-trailer see: www.youtube.com/watch?v=kbjXz4mx8Bk.

[33] www.classictic.com/zh/turangalîla__festspielhaus_baden-baden/77296/.

[34] https://vimeo.com/244432996, www.assiscarreiro.com/andrew-mcnicol.

by the Belgrade Philharmonic Orchestra conducted by Zivojim Zdravkovic (Geerard Patris, director; 1965); and a UK documentary from the television series *The Lively Arts* presented by Robin Ray and featuring the London Symphony Orchestra and André Previn (Barrie Gavin, director; 1977).[35] The entire fifth movement was used in conductor Simon Rattle's TV series *Leaving Home: Orchestral Music in the 20th Century* (Volume 2: Rhythm), broadcast in 1996.[36]

8 Concluding Remarks

Messiaen's analysis in his *Traité* clearly demonstrates that there is much more to the symphony than might be inferred by his brief program notes for the premiere. No program notes can completely account for what occurs in a piece of complex music, and his notes from 1949 are typical of their time; however, a preconcert lecture combined with a well-conceived visual presentation would enhance the audience's appreciation for and enjoyment of the piece, especially for the first-time listener.

Messiaen wanted people to hear detail. He understood that this was nigh impossible without studying the score; but as is described throughout his analysis and in his revised score, he pays special attention to making some of his mathematical procedures audible through timbre. For those reading the *Traité* he also expects a certain familiarity with his music or his sources, although he is also careful to explain some compositional techniques such as his rhythmic characters and his adaptation of Hindu rhythms.

Messiaen also wanted his music to make an impression:

> It's not essential for listeners to be able to detect precisely all the rhythmic procedures of the music they hear, just as they don't need to figure out all the chords of classical music. That's reserved for harmony professors and professional composers. The moment that they receive a shock, realize that it's beautiful, that the music touches them, the goal is achieved! (Samuel 1994: 83).

He had previously suggested a similar way to listen to his music:

> Let us now think of the listener[s] of our modal and rhythmic music; [they] will not have time at the concert to inspect the nontranspositions and nonretrogradations, and, at that moment these questions will not interest [them] further; to be charmed will be their only desire. And that is precisely what will happen; in spite of themselves, they will submit to the strange charm of impossibilities … which will lead them progressively to that sort of theological rainbow which the musical language attempts to be (Messiaen, 1944: 21).

---

[35] www.imdb.com/title/tt7728628/?ref_=fn_tt_tt_10,
www.imdb.com/title/tt11635288/?ref_=fn_tt_tt_3.
[36] www.imdb.com/title/tt0379127/?ref_=ttep_ep_tt.

Far more difficult than comprehending the various musical techniques at work is making sense of the program. It is really only in the *Traité* that Messiaen provides elaboration on the aspects of these stories that interest him, and which are encapsulated in his music. Rarely, though, are these explicit; rather, they are surreal juxtapositions of images from which we individually assemble our own narrative. Since Messiaen did not leave a complete and detailed description of how the Tristan myth is revealed, explained, or expanded in his works, there is perhaps limited value in trying to fill in the gaps, especially given that even if we did have full information, it should not interfere with our personal experience of the music. Perhaps we can conclude, as musicologist Paul Griffiths did, that "ultimately, . . . the work is not made to be understood, but made rather to draw its listeners through mind-defying complexity, alterations of time sense and sheer brilliance into a state of amazement (Griffiths, 1985: 139)."

It is almost impossible to hear Messiaen's music with clean ears (i.e., without any knowledge of the title or program or having read any notes or descriptions) that would allow a listener to hear the work and formulate their own original response. The problem is that, if we believe that the only real way to listen to Messiaen's music is to devote time and energy to understanding it in its technical and programmatic complexity, then we run the risk of forcing it out of the canon. At best, Messiaen's commentaries give us permission to embrace the images the music naturally makes for each of us and perhaps provide the inspiration to listen more often and more closely. The *Turangalîla-symphonie*, though, is quite remarkable in many respects and counts as a masterwork of musical surrealism that deserves to be played and heard for its love and for its joy.

References

Baeck, E. (2017). André Cluytens et les "Trois Tâla" d'Olivier Messiaen. *Revue Belge de Musicologie/Belgisch Tijdschrift voor Muziekwetenschap*, 71, 153–179.

Bédier, J. (1924). *Le Roman de Tristan et Iseult*. Paris: Éditions d'Art.

Bernard, J. W. (1986). Messiaen's Synaesthesia: The Correspondence between Color and Sound Structure in His Music. *Music Perception*, 4, 41–68.

Bradbury, W. C. (1991). Messiaen and Gamelan: An Analysis of Gamelan in the *Turangalîla-symphonie*. Cornell University, PhD dissertation.

Bruhn, S. (2008). *Messiaen's Explorations of Love and Death: Musico-Poetic Signification in the "Tristan Trilogy" and Three Related Song Cycles*. Hillsdale, NY: Pendragon Press.

Byrne, B. P. (2009). An Exploration of the Cyclic Themes in Olivier Messiaen's *Turangalila-symphonie*. Boston University, MA thesis.

Cheong, W.-L. (2003). Messiaen's Chord Tables: Ordering the Disordered. *Tempo*, 57(226), 2–10.

Davidson, A. E. (2001). *Olivier Messiaen and the Tristan Myth*. Westport, CT: Prager.

Fallon, R. (2007). The Record of Realism in Messiaen's Bird Style. In C. Dingle and N. Simeone, eds. *Olivier Messiaen: Music, Art and Literature*. Burlington, VT: Ashgate.

Fancher, J. E. (2003). Pitch Organization in the *Turangalîla-symphonie* of Olivier Messiaen. University of Minnesota, PhD dissertation.

Goléa, A. (1961). *Rencontres avec Olivier Messiaen*. Paris: R. Julliard.

Griffiths, P. (1985). *Olivier Messiaen and the Music of Time*. Ithaca, NY: Cornell University Press.

Guth, P. (1953). Nébuleuses spirales, stalactites et stalagmites suggèrent des rythmes à Olivier Messiaen. *Le Figaro Littéraire* (February 14), 4.

Hayes, M. 1995. Instrumental and Choral Works to 1948. In P. Hill, ed. *The Messiaen Companion*. Portland, OR: Amadeus Press.

Hill, P., and Simeone, N. (2005). *Messiaen*. New Haven, CT: Yale University Press.

Hook, J. L. (1998). Rhythm in the Music of Messiaen: An Algebraic Study and an Application in the *Turangalîla Symphony*. *Music Theory Spectrum*, 20(1), 97–120.

Kraft, D. (2013). *Birdsong in the Music of Olivier Messiaen*. South Carolina: Arosa Press.

McNeill, R. (2010). Messiaen's *Turangalîla-symphonie* and Its Place within the Symphonic Genre of the First Half of the Twentieth Century. In J. Crisp, ed., *Olivier Messiaen: The Centenary Papers*. Newcastle upon Tyne: Cambridge Scholars Publishing, 103–204.

Messiaen, O. (1935). *La Nativité du Seigneur*. Paris, Leduc.

Messiaen, O. (1942). *Quatuor pour la fin du Temps*. Paris, Durand.

Messiaen, O. (1944). *Technique de mon langage musical*. 2 volumes (volume 1: text; volume 2: music examples). Paris: Leduc. Volume 1 translated by John Satterfield as *The Technique of My Musical Language*. Paris: Leduc, 1956.

Messiaen, O. (1948). *Harawi*. Paris: Leduc.

Messiaen, O. (1949a). *Cinq rechants*. Paris: Salabert.

Messiaen, O. (1949b). Program for BSO premiere of *Turangalîla-symphonie*. Boston: BSO Publications.

Messiaen, O. (1953/1994). *Turangalîla-symphonie*. Paris: Durand.

Messiaen, O. (1991). Liner notes to *Olivier Messiaen, Turangalîla-symphonie*. Translated by Paul Griffiths (Deutsche Grammophon 431781–2).

Messiaen, O. (1995). *Traité de rythme, de couleur, et d'ornithologie*. Volume 2, Paris: Leduc.

Messiaen, O. (1996). *Traité de rythme, de couleur, et d'ornithologie*. Volume 3, Paris: Leduc.

Milsom, J. (1995). Organ Music I. In P. Hill, ed., *The Messiaen Companion*. London: Faber & Faber, 51–71.

Peterson, L. (1998). Messiaen and Surrealism: A Study of His Poetry. In S. Bruhn, ed., *Messiaen's Language of Mystical Love*. New York: Garland Publishing, 215–224.

Pople, A. (1995). Messiaen's Musical Language: An Introduction. In P. Hill, ed. *The Messiaen Companion*. London: Faber & Faber, 15–50.

Samuel, C. (1986). *Olivier Messiaen: Musique et couleur*. Paris: Belfond. Translated by E. Thomas Glasow as *Olivier Messiaen: Music and Color: Conversations with Claude Samuel*. Portland, OR: Amadeus Press, 1994.

Schweizer, K. (1982). *Olivier Messiaen, Turangalîla-symphonie*. Munich: W. Fink Verlag.

Shenton, A. (2007). Composer as Performer, Recording as Text: Notes Towards a "Manner of Realization" for Messiaen's Music. In R. Sholl, ed. *Messiaen Studies*. Cambridge, UK: Cambridge University Press, 168–187.

Sherlaw Johnson, R. (1975). *Messiaen*. Berkeley, CA: University of California Press.

Sholl, R. (2007). Love, Mad Love and the "*point sublime*": The Surrealist Poetics of Messiaen's *Harawi*. In R. Sholl, ed. *Messiaen Studies*. Cambridge, UK: Cambridge University Press, 34–62.

Simeone, N. (2002). An Exotic Tristan in Boston: The First Performance of Messiaen's *Turangalîla-symphonie*. In R. Barber, ed. *King Arthur in Music*. Cambridge, UK: D. S. Brewer.

Simeone, N. (2007). Dancing *Turangalîla*: Messiaen and the Ballet. In C. Dingle and N. Simeone, eds., *Olivier Messiaen: Music, Art, Literature*. Aldershot: Ashgate, 289–300.

Simeone, N. (2008). Messiaen, Koussevitzky and the USA. *The Musical Times*, 149 (1905), 25–44.

Acknowledgments

I wish to acknowledge with gratitude the staff of the music library at Boston University for assisting me with finding materials; my research assistant, Vaughn Nelson, whose thorough investigative and editing skills were invaluable; my colleague Nigel Simeone for bringing his enormous knowledge of the subject and his meticulous eye to the manuscript; Bridget P. Carr, Blanche and George Jones Director of Archives and Digital Collections at the Boston Symphony Orchestra, for providing me access to their materials and for assisting with permissions; Samuel Nelson for his meticulous typesetting of the music; Mervyn Cooke and Kate Brett at Cambridge University Press for their confidence in the project; and to the Boston University Center for the Humanities for its financial support. Finally, this Element is dedicated, with affection and admiration, to Lynanne B. Wescott, Esq.

Permissions

Musical examples from the symphony © 1949 Éditions Durand, a catalogue of Universal Music Publishing Classical, International Copyright Secured, All Rights Reserved, reprinted by permission of Hal Leonard Europe BV(Italy). Quotations from the second volume of *Traité De Rythme, De Couleur, Et D'Ornithologie, tome II* by Olivier Messiaen Copyright © 1995 Première Music Group – Catalogue ALPHONSE LEDUC EDITIONS MUSICALES, International Copyright Secured, All Rights Reserved, reprinted by Permission of Hal Leonard Europe Ltd.

Figure 1 file available at <https://commons.wikimedia.org/wiki/File:Ondes_martenot.jpg>; license available at <www.gnu.org/licenses/fdl-1.3.html>

Figure 2 file available at <https://publicdomainreview.org/collection/details-from-bosch-s-garden-of-earthly-delights-ca-1500/>; license available at <https://creativecommons.org/publicdomain/mark/1.0/>

Figure 3 file available at <https://en.wikipedia.org/wiki/File:Mona_Lisa,_by_Leonardo_da_Vinci,_from_C2RMF_retouched.jpg>; license available at <https://commons.wikimedia.org/w/index.php?title=Commons:PD&redirect=no>

Figure 4 Digital Image © 2022 Artists Rights Society (ARS), New York / ADAGP, Paris.

Figure 5 file available at <https://commons.wikimedia.org/wiki/File: Giovanni_Battista_Piranesi,_The_Drawbridge,_1780s,_NGA_9788.jpg>; license available at <https://creativecommons.org/publicdomain/zero/1.0/deed.en>

Figure 6 file, available at <https://commons.wikimedia.org/wiki/File: Great_Sphinx_of_Giza_-_20080716a.jpg>; license available at <www.gnu .org/licenses/fdl-1.3.html>

Figure 7 file available at <https://commons.wikimedia.org/wiki/File: Temple_of_the_warriors_chichen_itza.jpg>; license; available at <www.gnu .org/licenses/fdl-1.3.html>

Figure 8 file available at <https://commons.wikimedia.org/wiki/File: Tumba_de_pakal,_Chiapas.JPG>; license available at <https://creative commons.org/licenses/by-sa/3.0/deed.en>

Figure 9 file available at <https://commons.wikimedia.org/wiki/File: Tomb_of_Xiao_Xiu_-_P1200169.JPG>; license available at <https://creative commons.org/licenses/by-sa/3.0/deed.en>

Figure 10 file available at <https://commons.wikimedia.org/wiki/File: CoiledSnakeNorthAltar.JPG>; license available at <https://en.wikipedia.org/ wiki/Public_domain>

Figure 11 file available at <https://commons.wikimedia.org/wiki/File:Ahu-Tongariki-2013.jpg>; license available at <https://creativecommons.org/ licenses/by-sa/3.0/deed.en>

Figure 12 image © Andrew Shenton.

Figures 13, 14, 15 images © Andrew Shenton, content reproduced by kind permission of the Boston Symphony Orchestra Archives <http://collections .bso.org/digital/> (BSO Archives; MGT 205; Messiaen).

Cambridge Elements ☰

Music Since 1945

Mervyn Cooke
University of Nottingham

Mervyn Cooke brings to the role of series editor an unusually broad range of expertise, having published widely in the fields of twentieth-century opera, concert and theatre music, jazz, and film music. He has edited and co-edited *Cambridge Companions to Britten, Jazz, Twentieth-Century Opera*, and *Film Music*. His other books include *Britten: War Requiem, Britten and the Far East, A History of Film Music, The Hollywood Film Music Reader, Pat Metheny: The ECM Years*, and two illustrated histories of jazz. He is currently co-editing (with Christopher R. Wilson) *The Oxford Handbook of Shakespeare and Music*.

About the Series

Elements in Music Since 1945 is a highly stimulating collection of authoritative online Elements that reflects the latest research into a wide range of musical topics of international significance since the Second World War. Individual Elements are organised into constantly evolving clusters devoted to such topics as art music, jazz, music and image, stage and screen genres, music and media, music and place, immersive music, music and movement, music and politics, music and conflict, and music and society. The latest research questions in theory, criticism, musicology, composition and performance are also given cutting-edge and thought-provoking coverage. The digital-first format allows authors to respond rapidly to new research trends, with contributions being updated to reflect the latest thinking in their fields, and the Elements are enhanced by the provision of an exciting range of online resources.

Cambridge Elements ≡

Music Since 1945

Elements in the Series

Music Transforming Conflict
Ariana Phillips-Hutton

Herbert Eimert and the Darmstadt School: The Consolidation of the Avant-Garde
Max Erwin

Baroque Music in Post-War Cinema: Performance Practice and Musical Style
Donald Greig

A Semiotic Approach to Open Notations: Ambiguity as Opportunity
Tristan McKay

Film Music in Concert: The Pioneering Role of the Boston Pops Orchestra
Emilio Audissino

Theory of Prominence: Temporal Structure of Music Based on Linguistic Stress
Bryan Hayslett

Heiner Goebbels and Curatorial Composing after Cage
Ed McKeon

Understanding Stockhausen
Robin Maconie

Olivier Messiaen's Turangalîla-symphonie
Andrew Shenton

A full series listing is available at: www.cambridge.org/em45

Printed in the United States
by Baker & Taylor Publisher Services